HOW TO
GET A
GREAT JOB

A Library How-To Handbook

Editors of the
American Library Association

Skyhorse Publishing

Skyhorse Publishing books may be purchased in bulk at special discounts for sales promotion, corporate gifts, fund-raising, or educational purposes. Special editions can also be created to specifications. For details, contact the Special Sales Department, Skyhorse Publishing, 307 West 36th Street, 11th Floor, New York, NY 10018 or info@skyhorsepublishing.com.

Skyhorse® and Skyhorse Publishing® are registered trademarks of Skyhorse Publishing, Inc.®, a Delaware corporation.

www.skyhorsepublishing.com

10 9 8 7 6 5 4 3 2 1

Library of Congress Cataloging-in-Publication Data

How to get a great job : a library how-to handbook / by editors of the American Library Association.
    p. cm.
Includes bibliographical references and index.
ISBN 978-1-61608-154-6 (pbk. : alk. paper)
1. Job hunting. 2. Libraries and the unemployed. 3. Unemployed--Services for. 4. Vocational guidance. I. American Library Association.
HF5382.7.H68 2011
650.14--dc22

                                2010047819

ALA ISBN: 978-0-8389-1076-4

Printed in China

Contents

"Beyond the Books" in Today's Public Libraries

Are you aware of all the resources that your public library offers "beyond the books"? Today's community libraries offer a lot more than books, audiobooks, and movies to check out. You can attend a free workshop or lecture, browse online resources that aren't available anywhere else, and use your library's computers and software programs to prepare for a test or master a new skill—all for free.

CHECK IT OUT!

You probably used public library resources as a grade-schooler, and are familiar with the basics of locating a specific book or magazine. (If you're not, ask a librarian for help—you'll relearn this very quickly!) But you should also be aware of these basics offered by any public library today:

Interlibrary loan:

If your library doesn't have the book or resource you want, you may be able to borrow it from another branch or library system through interlibrary loan. It's easy to use, and you can pick up your requested materials at your local library.

Reference section:

Generally, reference materials are not available for checkout, but you can browse, read, and photocopy them in the library. The *Occupational Outlook Handbook* is a good example.

Computer stations:

Your library may require that you reserve a computer, that you limit your time to a half hour or hour at a time, or that you use certain computers for certain tasks. (Some libraries have computers dedicated to homework or to job searches.) Check the rules before you sit down.

Internet access:

Your library is likely to offer wireless Internet access in addition to computer stations. In this case, you can bring your laptop computer (or see if library laptops are available for checkout), find a comfortable seat, and surf the job sites for free.

Subscription databases:

You'll read about specific databases in this book that can give your search a boost. Public and school libraries have paid subscriptions to various comprehensive online databases of job-search information that simply aren't available anywhere else.

Specialty librarians:

Depending on the size of your library system, librarians specializing in jobs and careers may be available in your local branch or elsewhere within the library system.

Public libraries routinely offer free classes, tutorials, workshops, and other educational programs. Job-search topics may include résumé writing, basic computer skills, interviewing, and more.

LIBRARIES AND JOB-SEEKERS

Part of the mission of any public library is to meet the needs of its community. So, beyond stocking resources to help students with school-work; providing books, magazines, and newspapers for entertainment and information; and offering Internet access to the public, your library should be doing *something* to help local job-seekers find work. How much it offers will depend on the library's budget, available resources, and innovation. Many libraries are relying on volunteers and partnerships with local employment groups to provide workshops or one-on-one help, or providing a meeting space for a job support group. Others may simply be adding books, software programs, and subscription databases that can help with job research.

Find out what your local library is doing—no matter how scant the available resources there, the research expertise of librarians, the information and lists already compiled, and the print and online materials available are sure to save you time and money while you look for a great job.

ASK AND YE SHALL RECEIVE

What if your library is small, understaffed, or simply doesn't offer much for job-seekers? You can request that resources be added. If the library has a suggestion box or the online equivalent, use it. If not, ask for the name of the head of the reference section, and write that person a letter or e-mail. However you request additional materials, be specific about what you want. You don't need to know the exact resource; you can state your need:

"I would like to be able to practice interviewing for a job with someone who can give me objective, concrete advice and feedback."

"I am studying to take the GED, and understand there are software programs to help with this. If the library could provide a program for community use, that would really help me."

"I know that some libraries around the country are offering résumé workshops. Our library should add this type of workshop."

SIX SIMPLE STEPS

For people who haven't used a public library much lately, these should be the first steps you take:

1. If you don't already have a library card, get one. All it takes is a photo ID and proof of address—check with your library to find out exactly what's required. A library card is free, but it acts as the "membership card" that's needed to access materials, including online databases you can search from home, interlibrary loans, and, of course, books, DVDs, and other materials for checkout.

2. Visit your library's website to explore the resources it offers. Browse the entire site to get an overview, and then see if there is a special webpage or section devoted to job search, career help, etc.

3. Go to your library in person to talk to a librarian. Explain that you are looking for help with a job search, and ask if there is a jobs and career specialist, a general business librarian, or a reference librarian who would be the best person to talk to about your search.

4. Some libraries let you schedule an appointment to talk one-on-one with a specific librarian for a set amount of time. If your library does this, by all means make an appointment! If not, find out when your chosen librarian has some time to talk to you.

5. Ask what resources are available to help you, including compilations of job websites, databases, workshops or classes, résumé review, etc. Your library may also offer lists of community resources that can help you.

6. Finally, learn how to physically find the resources—books, periodicals, reference materials, etc.—that you'll be using in your search. Explore your library and note where job-search information can be found.

THE LAST WORD

Libraries are continually changing and adding to the resources they offer. Even in times of tight budgets and reduced staff, they will find ways to share information, even if it is simply a photocopied list of local resources or websites on a specific topic. So if you think you know what your library has to offer for your job search based on what you found last year—don't be too sure. Head straight back to the reference desk and check out what's new.

Before You Begin

Think of this chapter as laying the groundwork for a successful job search. Before you update your résumé, click on your first "apply now" link on an online posting, or pick up the phone to call a former coworker for a job lead. Take the time to make sure you're prepared.

Following all the advice in this chapter should take some people as little as an hour, and others no more than a day—not a bad investment for something as important as finding a great job!

Best in Show—General Websites

Job-hunt, www.job-hunt.org.
The Riley Guide, www.rileyguide.com.
Toronto Public Library, "Career and Job Search Help Blog,"

http://torontopubliclibrary.typepad.com/jobhelp.

The Wall Street Journal, "Careers," www.careerjournal.com.

Weddle's, www.weddles.com. Sign up for the free e-newsletter *WEDDLE's Newsletter For Job Seekers & Career Activists* at www.weddles.com/seekernews/index.cfm.

WetFeet, www.wetfeet.com.

Quintessential Careers, www.quintcareers.com.

LIBRARY RESOURCES

Check Out Your Library

We may be biased, but your public library has valuable resources you can use to start your search that will help out for its duration. You're likely to find the job-search information you're looking for already neatly compiled, along with knowledgeable help and guidance, free computer and Internet use, and perhaps even valuable workshops and meetings.

"I think people want individual attention," says librarian Bonnie Easton of the people who come to her Career Center at the Cuyahoga County (Ohio) Public Library. "They want some sense that they're going in the right direction. This is hard to figure out when you're on your own."

Jerome L. Myers, MLS, the main library manager at the Tacoma (Washington) Public Library's Education and Job Center, adds, "The first thing job-seekers have to do is look into what they want to do and figure out the career they want. This is a great place to start."

INVENTORY YOUR CONTACT INFORMATION

As soon as you get the word out that you're looking for work, you should be ready for potential employers and your extended network to contact you. So before you contact anyone, take an inventory of the ways *they* can contact *you*:

1. Your E-mail Address

You'll need an address to sign in to many websites, to include in online job applications, and so that employers can communicate with you. Make sure you use the same e-mail address for all your job-search activities. Consider setting up a separate account just for job-search-related communications; this will make it easier to track your search. Just remember to check that in-box frequently!

> **TIP:** NEVER USE YOUR WORK E-MAIL ADDRESS TO LOOK FOR A NEW JOB. NOT ONLY IS IT AN ABUSE OF YOUR EMPLOYER'S RESOURCES THAT CAN GET YOU IN TROUBLE, IT SENDS A TERRIBLE MESSAGE TO ANY POTENTIAL HIRERS.

Whatever e-mail address you decide to create or use, make sure it sounds professional. If you're currently found at tequilalover@freee-mail.com or adasmommy@hotmail.com, take a few minutes to create a second address for job-search communications.

Four Free E-mail Options

You can set up and use an e-mail account without spending a dime. Consider any of the following easy-to-use options for your job-search e-mail:

Gmail—http://mail.google.com

Offered through Google, with the side benefit of automatic access to Google Docs.

mail.com—www.mail.com

Choose from 250 different addresses, including @techie.com or @ accountant.com.

Yahoo! Mail—http://mail.yahoo.com

While Yahoo! doesn't seem as professional as Gmail or mail.com, it's easy to use and perfectly acceptable.

Windows Live Mail—http://mail.live.com

Formerly Hotmail, and still found at hotmail.com with @hotmail addresses.

Because they are web-based, these accounts can be accessed from any computer, anywhere, including the stations in your library.

2. Your Telephone

Before you draft a résumé or input contact information into a search site, decide which telephone number you're going to use throughout your search. (Again, don't even consider using your current work number.) Your cell phone is the most logical choice, because it is your personal number and completely in your control.

Listen to the voice mail recording on the phone you've chosen to make sure it sounds appropriate to potential employers who may hear it. Ditch any jokes or silliness, background music, and rambling. Rerecord it if necessary, to include your name ("You've reached the voice mail of . . .") and the promise to call back as soon as possible.

During your search, focus on professionalism every time your phone rings. Be careful to check the caller ID readout and, unless you are absolutely sure that you know the friend or family member who's calling, answer the call in a professional way, the way you might if you were already working at your great job: "Good morning, this is Jim."

3. Your Mailing Address

It's always been standard practice to include a street address on every résumé and cover letter—but consider whether you want to do this. If you think that sharing this information may be unnecessary or even harmful to your search—revealing an extralong commute may bring up doubts that you will stick with the job long-term, for example—you may want to avoid including a "snail mail" address.

Of course another option if you don't want to publicize your address, either to specific hirers or the entire Internet world, is investing in a PO box and using that as your job-search address.

4. Your Web Presence

Prepare to be Googled. One last "before you . . ." step in your pre–job search process: Browse the Internet to see what kind of presence you have. Search on your full name with and without your town (and town of employment) to see what comes up.

GOOD things include projects you've been involved with in your current and past jobs, your LinkedIn profile, and community activities.

BAD things include inappropriate remarks and photos posted by yourself or "friends" on Facebook. If your search turns up drunken poses, sexually suggestive comments, etc., try your best to have them removed. If a friend refuses to delete something from Facebook, ask that they change privacy settings so that only friends can see it.

Factoid

Microsoft commissioned an online reputation survey in 2009, in which 79 percent of U.S. hiring managers and job recruiters said they conducted online searches on job applicants. And 70 percent of those potential hirers stated that they had rejected a candidate based on what they found online!

ARM YOURSELF WITH BASIC SKILLS, SOFTWARE

The absolute basic skills needed for any job search now include the ability to use a computer well enough to find and fill out an online job application—which in turn will require an e-mail address. This is true even for positions that will never require you to use these skills on the job—including retail store workers and fast food restaurant employees.

If you're not comfortable using the Internet, your public library may be able to help. "You can learn basic computer skills here, and then learn every stage of the job search," says Jerome Myers, the main library manager at the Tacoma (Washington) Public Library's Education and Job Center.

WEB USE 101

If you're not familiar with using the Internet, you will be—your job search will teach you browsing skills fast! But here are some basics to keep in mind as you get started:

Logging In: Many job-search sites will require you to set up an account and then log in every time you want to check listings. Put some consideration into creating a user name and password for these sites.

Secure passwords use a combination of letters, numbers, and symbols. You can use the same user name and password for every job-search site to ensure you'll remember them.

> **TIP:** Your user name may be seen by the public, so choose something professional, just like your e-mail address.

CAPTCHA: Completely Automated Public Turing Test to Tell Computers and Humans Apart is the program that asks you to type in one or more words displayed as distorted images. This is becoming standard for many sites that require users to input personal information; it proves that the person entering the site is a real human being and not a web-crawling robot used to hack sites.

Protect Your Privacy: Check each job-search site (and résumé-writing service or other site that requires you to enter personal information) for a privacy policy. This is a legal document that outlines how your personal information may be used. Consider that you're typing in all sorts of information that can be used for unwanted solicitations and even identity theft.

Keep in mind that any information you post on sites, including your résumé, can be found and read by anyone—so be stingy with how much you share! This includes posting any contact information for your references.

RÉSUMÉ AND LETTER WRITING

In addition to an Internet connection, you'll need software to create and revise your résumé and cover letters. Microsoft Word is the most common, but there are specific programs for this. If you don't own Word and want a standard-format résumé, you can use Google Docs, a free online service that includes a résumé template. You simply type over the sample résumé to create your own, without purchasing or using any word-processing software. (https://docs.google.com/Doc?id=dghd5rk7_0hzd4bzfx)

You will also need to create PDFs. If you don't have Adobe Acrobat and you are using a Windows operating system, you can download free software called PDFCreator from http://sourceforge.net/projects/pdfcreator.

Again, if you don't have any of these programs, your public library can probably help.

> **TIP:** If you are creating or revising documents at a computer outside your home, buy a **USB** flash drive (also called a thumb drive or memory stick), and save all your documents on it so you'll always have them handy. Never save your personal documents to the hard drive of a computer you don't own!

And if you're creating your résumé while away from your home, make sure you bring (or have memorized) all the necessary information to be included, including dates of past employment.

Any additional software you might need would be for keeping your search organized, which is covered in the next section.

WORK YOUR PLAN

Aside from some basic computer knowledge, an Internet connection, and a couple of software programs, you need one more thing to begin your job search: a plan. Your plan should include:

1. A clear strategy on what you want in your next job and what you don't
2. A schedule to hold yourself accountable
3. Goals to keep your job search moving ahead
4. A system for tracking what you've done
5. A plan for improving your salability on the job market

TIP: YOUR JOB SEARCH IS LIKE A JOB IN ITSELF, SO MAKE IT SEEM LIKE ONE. CHOOSE AN AREA IN YOUR HOME AS YOUR "JOB-SEARCH OFFICE," AND KEEP ALL INFORMATION, FILES, AND SUPPLIES THERE, INCLUDING YOUR CALENDAR AND TO-DO LIST.

1. What Do You Want?

Take some time to think through what you are looking for. You should have a clear idea of what type(s) of positions you want and which you can realistically apply for. You should also calculate how much money you need to pay your bills and meet financial obligations (including savings) and how much you *want* to make. Other general "wants" might include

+ Location: How far are you willing to commute? Are you willing to relocate?
+ Does your family or personal life put any constraints on your work, such as inability to travel or need for flexible hours?
+ Are there any "must haves" to include in your search? These may include certain benefits, an option for working from home, or a certain level of management responsibilities.

2. Stick to a Schedule

Most full-time employees today have a forty-hour workweek. If you're out of work, that's how much time you should dedicate to your job search. If you're employed while you're job hunting, you'll have to find as much personal time as you can for your job search.

No matter what your employment situation, your first step is to figure out a realistic schedule for each day and each week that devotes plenty of time to researching, networking, and reading and answering ads for open positions. Then stick to that schedule. This can be the toughest part of any job search, but you can do it! Write your daily schedule in your calendar if necessary, or create a daily to-do list that includes your job-search steps. Or do both!

For example, in addition to a preset number of hours spent browsing job boards online, you might block out every Wednesday morning from 9 to 11 AM for research at your public library, and then dedicate Wednesday afternoon from 2 to 4 PM to commenting on online industry and job-search forums and blogs.

> **TIP: IF YOU ARE HAVING TROUBLE STICKING TO YOUR JOB SEARCH, ENLIST A COLLEAGUE OR FRIEND WHO WILL HOLD YOU ACCOUNTABLE. PERHAPS YOU CAN TEAM UP WITH SOMEONE IN YOUR JOB SUPPORT NETWORK, OR JUST A SUPPORTIVE FRIEND. SIMPLY TELLING SOMEONE WHAT YOU PLAN TO ACCOMPLISH TODAY (OR THIS WEEK) WILL GIVE YOU A NUDGE TO DO IT. IF NOT, HAVING THAT PERSON ASK YOU IF YOU COMPLETED WHAT YOU PLANNED SHOULD HELP YOU STAY ON SCHEDULE.**

Daily Job-Search To-Do List

+ Check your e-mail (at least twice a day)
+ Respond to any employer, recruiter, or networking contact who e-mails that same day
+ Check voice mail throughout the day if you're away from your phone
+ Log all jobs applied to, contacts talked to (or e-mailed), and events attended

3. Set Small Goals

Putting in the time is not the goal; getting results is. With this in mind, set specific goals for each day, week, and month. Rather than aiming for a certain number of jobs applied for—this will lead you to send applications or résumés for  unsuitable fits—set goals for new research sources found, the number of in-person networking events you'll attend, the number of telephone cold calls you'll make, etc.

At the end of each day and each week, note your progress. Did you meet your goals? What were the results you gleaned? If you find that your goals were set too high (or too low), adjust them accordingly for the days and weeks ahead.

4. Get Organized

Your job-search plan must include an organizational system. This includes the schedule (with daily and weekly to-do lists) and goals you've set up, along with ways to keep track of what you've done. This is much easier if you "log in" each activity as soon as you've completed it.

Keep Records

Later in this book you'll get specific information on what types of records to keep, but you should be prepared from the start to record every position you apply for, every promising contact you make through networking, and every step that follows either of these.

You can keep your records electronically or on paper, but you'll need a system that alerts you about when (and how) to follow up, and helps you remember which résumé went to which company.

If you've already started your job search, go through every application or résumé you've turned in and try to reconstruct what you've done.

Organize Your Files

As you'll find out in chapters 4 and 5, you're going to end up with multiple versions of your résumé and cover letter. You'll want to save these so that you can retrieve them in the event that you get a callback about an opening you applied for, or simply because you want to re–revise a certain version of your résumé.

All these documents should be saved electronically; there is no reason to print out every version. Devise a naming system for your files that is easily scannable and understandable, and keep everything in a folder such as "Résumés." This should be placed in another folder with any other job-search documentation you may acquire.

If you prefer, you can store your résumés and letters online, using Google Documents (http://docs.google.com). This free system lets you upload documents and then access them from any computer with an Internet connection anywhere.

If you find it difficult to work with a completely computer-based system, you can keep notes of which résumé went to which job ad by either printing out a spreadsheet (covered in chapter 3) or writing it out in longhand.

Track Your Expenses

As part of your general organizational system, keep track of any expenses related to your job search. The costs of getting business cards printed, mileage and parking fees for interviews, phone calls, and much more may all be tax deductible. The IRS states, "You can deduct certain expenses you have in looking for a new job in your present occupation, even if you do not get a new job." Note that expenses related to looking for a job in a *new* field are not deductible.

5. Get Skilled

Are there skills you need to acquire in order to apply for your dream job? What about skills that may boost your income level? If you know of something that will give  you an edge in your job hunt—like learning a new software program or understanding the key concepts in an emerging trend—devote some of your time to learning it. You may be able to do this by reading, by taking a class or practice exam at your local library, or through volunteer work.

FINAL STEP: GET CONNECTED

Looking for a job can be lonely work—especially if you're unemployed and cut off from the busy work environment you're used to. To stay connected to the professional world, get the support and advice you need, and get out of the house, find a job-search club or a networking support group. (See chapter 6.) A group like this will provide emotional support, and you'll be able to share advice and even your contacts with other members.

If you can't find a group you like, consider starting your own—or you can go the online route with a group on Meetup.com, Yahoo! Groups, or Google Groups. But don't let your online relationships be your only support—you should also regularly ask friends, former coworkers, and new networking contacts to meet you for a cup of coffee or a walk around the park. Discuss your job search, ask for ideas, or simply catch up on news from the "outside world."

THE LAST WORD

You will almost certainly revise your job-search plan as you go. Once you have spent some time in the trenches looking for a job, you'll have a better understanding of the commitments, activities, and results involved. This should lead you to add and revise goals, shift your schedule around, and tweak your organizational system. This is fine— just be sure that you are working as hard as you need to in order to find a great job!

CHAPTER 2

Researching the Job Market

Before you start your job search (or get any further with the one you're in the midst of), take some time to put your search in a larger context. Every job-seeker should know the "lay of the land" for his targeted industry or profession. Start by asking yourself these questions:

+ Do you know the titles or descriptions of positions you should be applying for?
+ What is the current outlook for the jobs you're seeking in your geographic region?
+ Do you have the appropriate qualifications for the level and type of job(s) you're searching for?
+ Are there other industries or positions you might be qualified for that you should include in your search?

✦ And finally, if the outlook for your targeted industry/positions is not good, can you find a different profession that might be easier to be hired into? If so, what will it take?

You can improve your odds of finding great jobs that match your qualifications by starting out with a broader search. As you research the job market and review job postings, look at *all* types of jobs within your targeted industry or industries, and see what is available. If this becomes too overwhelming, you can begin to narrow your search by eliminating certain positions or other criteria from your search.

FOR INSTANCE . . .

"Lateral" moves like the examples below don't involve a complete career change; they simply stretch the options for using the skills and experience a professional has already acquired:

✦ daycare worker to teacher's assistant
✦ telemarketer to receptionist
✦ office manager to computer tech support
✦ ad agency graphic designer to account representative (or vice versa)
✦ high-speed Internet installer to high-speed Internet customer-service rep

You may need to sell yourself a little more strongly in your résumé and interviews to convince an employer that your experience will translate.

"If you read the odds of your résumé getting you an interview, it's depressing. Statistics are always against you—but just keep at it. Your qualifications will be a perfect match for a job somewhere, and they'll find you, if you just do the homework."

—Bernice Kao, job/career specialist and job service outreach librarian at Fresno County (California) Public Library

Best in Show—Occupation/Career Listings Online

The **Riley Guide's Career Research Center** at http://rileyguide.com/careers/index.shtml. "This library includes job descriptions, salary data and employment statistics, and education information for over 160 occupations!"

The **Vocational Information Center's** www.khake.com/page5.html offers lots of valuable links to sites with employment trends, state-by-state labor market information, economic statistics, and more.

Job-posting aggregator **Indeed.com** adds statistics for a dozen industries each month, providing at-a-glance information on where the jobs are. Click on "trends" from the home page to get started.

GET AN INDUSTRY SNAPSHOT

So what do you need to learn about your industry in order to shape your search? Your industry or profession snapshot should include answers to questions such as:

How is the industry's overall economic health? What is the forecast for job growth in the field? What is the unemployment rate within the industry? Are the companies that are major players doing well in the stock market?

What's happening in your neighborhood? Which organizations are located in your city or county? Are they hiring? Is growth in your area increasing or decreasing?

What's on the horizon in D.C.? Is there any pending legislation that will affect your industry's trends or economic health? (For example, the Homebuyer Tax Credit in 2008 and 2009 gave real estate a short-term boost.)

What are the trends? What does the business press have to say about your industry? Are there new technologies, new organizations, or changes in the business world that will affect your career?

YOUR FIRST STOP: THE LIBRARY'S INFORMATION COUNTER

Public libraries serve their communities—and if your community's needs include help with job-searching, your library should be able to provide information and resources to help with your research. Check your library's website for job or career pages, and stop by the reference desk to see what type of help is available. You may find that a librarian has already created a ready-to-use list of Internet resources you can get started with, or you may be able to access the library's information databases to gather information.

> "Right now, we're seeing more interest in career planning. As jobs are disappearing, people are seeking new industries with better demand."
>
> **—Bonnie Easton, librarian at the Career Center of the Cuyahoga County (Ohio) Public Library**

HIT THE BOOKS (ONLINE)

The federal government compiles industry information every year in volumes that are now available online for free. These are absolute "musts" to include in your research:

1. **Occupational Outlook Handbook (OOH)** Published by the U.S. Bureau of Labor Statistics (BLS), this guide should be available at your library in print, and can be found online at www.bls.gov/oco. Revised and updated every two years, it includes detailed career information for all types of occupations, including a description of what workers do on the job, training and education needed, expected job prospects, salaries or wages, and working conditions. You'll also find links to information on state-by-state job markets, job-search tips, and more.

2. **Career Guide to Industries (CGI)** A companion to the Occupational Outlook Handbook, this BLS publication is only available online, at www.bls.gov/oco/cg. It is similar to the OOH, and provides information on careers by industry, including occupations in the industry, expected job prospects, training and advancement, earnings, and more.

3. **Occupational Outlook Quarterly** An online quarterly magazine published by the BLS that covers a variety of career topics, such as new and emerging occupations, training opportunities, salary trends, and results of new studies from the BLS. The "magazine" is available at www.bls.gov/opub/ooq/ooqhome.htm.

4. **O*NET Online** Visit http://online.onetcenter.org to browse the O*NET OnLine database of occupational information. The Occupational Information Network (O*NET) is sponsored by the U.S. Department of Labor/Employment and Training Administration, and the database is a user-friendly resource with information on nearly 1,000 occupations. Browse by occupation or by skills. (How can I use my teaching skills and desire to help people?) There is a lot of information and a lot of ways to search or find it—so take some time to click around O*NET.

FIVE MORE RESOURCES

There are other outstanding sources for up-to-date information. Check these additional online and print sources for details on your industry and/or career:

1. **Wetfeet.com** offers its own insights and information on trends, major players, and job descriptions in major industries, as well as career information, at www.wetfeet.com/careers—industries.aspx.

2. **The Career Project** (thecareerproject.org) is a site that provides a brief description of thousands of jobs—from the workers themselves. Select an industry, and see comments from actual people working in it. Better yet, you can ask any of these "mentors" a

question via e-mail if you want more information on the kind of work they do (or money they make).

3. Another place to check is the listing of "**Best Jobs in America 2009**" at http://money.cnn.com/magazines/moneymag/bestjobs/2009/snapshots/1.html. You won't exactly find the "best" jobs, but you can see those with the most growth, highest pay, and highest rated quality of life.

4. The websites or member publications of any professional associations related to your chosen work. Associations will report—either directly or indirectly—on trends, pending and current legislation, and other factors that influence jobs in the field.

5. For general business information that may affect your chosen industry, browse these well-known publications online or in print at your public library:

Wall Street Journal (http://online.wsj.com/home-page)
Fortune (http://money.cnn.com/magazines/fortune/)
Fast Company (www.fastcompany.com)
Forbes (www.forbes.com)

ENTRY-LEVEL WORKERS AND CAREER-CHANGERS

If you are planning to change careers—or are just starting out in your first career—you'll face your own unique challenges. Job-seekers in these two categories are similar, because a complete change in careers can put an experienced professional back at the starting gate, looking for entry-level jobs. An employer is unlikely to give you credit—or a salary increase—because of past experience that will not translate to your new job.

Change Rule

To be clear, changing careers refers to a complete shift to a new industry, requiring different skills or knowledge from your previous positions. A legal secretary who wants to become a teacher is changing careers; a legal secretary who wants to become a paralegal is not.

Whether you're a new graduate, a mom reentering the workplace after a multiyear hiatus, or simply want to change careers, you're in for a lot of research. You need to figure out three things:

1. Where the jobs are
2. What you *really* want to do
3. How to make it happen

You know about the first item—just follow the advice for all job-seekers at the beginning of this chapter: head to the library, hit the web, and research the job markets. Don't choose a profession simply because the employment outlook is good! Training to become a nurse just for the guaranteed job security is sure to lead to unhappiness, stress, and possibly bad patient care if you're not suited for the work. So head back to the library, because the second item may take some additional research.

TAKING APTITUDE AND ASSESSMENT TESTS

An assessment test or career aptitude test can reveal what specific jobs might best suit your abilities, interests, and personality. Ask a librarian what the library—and the Internet—has to offer in this area.

The most widely know assessment tests are the Myers-Briggs Type Indicator, the Strong Interest Inventory, and the Campbell Interest &

Skill Survey, but there are dozens of them. Some library subscription databases include assessment tests. For example, "Gale's Testing and Educational Database includes many employment and aptitude tests that are very useful," says Jim DeArmey, coordinator of information services at Baltimore County (Maryland) Public Library.

The results of your aptitude or assessment test(s) should give you some specific ideas on careers to pursue. If the results simply outline your skills and aptitudes, match those up with the skills listed in the O*NET OnLine database to find careers. (That website again is http://online.onetcenter.org.)

GAINING SKILLS AND QUALIFICATIONS

Finally, you need to determine what qualifications you need to begin working in your chosen career. If you need some experience, look for an internship or volunteer position or project that might apply. (A librarian can help with this!) Perhaps you need to take a class—or earn an entire degree. Maybe you need to learn new skills or specific business expertise, or will have to pass an industry-specific exam. Again, the library may be able to help. Many libraries own software that teaches or tests specific skills—from an extensive program on studying for the GED, to learning Spanish, to a practice exam for master carpentry.

Jerome L. Myers, MLS, main library manager at the Tacoma (Washington) Public Library Education and Job Center, says, "There are certain careers that require applicants to pass a test, whether it's for air traffic control or typing skills. The civil service job exams are our most popular—for employment as a postal worker or police officer, for example. You can come to the library—or log in from home if you have a library card—and take a practice exam. You can work at your own pace; it's very beneficial."

Best in Show—Changing Careers

Jansen, Julie. *I Don't Know What I Want, But I Know It's Not This: A Step-by-Step Guide to Finding Gratifying Work.* (New York: Penguin, 2003).

Tieger, Paul, and Barbara Barron. *Do What You Are: Discover the Perfect Career for You Through the Secrets of Personality Type.* (New York: Little, Brown, 2007).

Lore, Nicholas. *The Pathfinder: How to Choose or Change Your Career for a Lifetime of Satisfaction and Success.* (New York: Simon and Schuster, Fireside, 1998).

STUDY YOUR SUBJECT

You'll see this same advice at various points within this book: research your target industry. Make it part of your job-search research to stay abreast of what's happening. Don't wait until you have an interview lined up—do it now so that while you're networking, or leaving a comment on an industry insider's blog, or meeting your new neighbor who happens to be a head-hunter, you're knowledgeable, up to date, and prepared with facts.

" "Do your own research. It's in the newspaper every single day."

—Bernice Kao, job/career specialist and job service outreach librarian at Fresno County (California) Public Library

You should know

- ✦ Major players in your industry and/or region—the organizations and perhaps the people who run them.
- ✦ Any recent changes to those major players. Mergers, moves, new products introduced, or headline-making news.
- ✦ The latest trends. By monitoring professional associations' websites and publications, relevant news sources, blogs, and LinkedIn groups, you'll see patterns emerge—those are the trends.
- ✦ Industry lingo, acronyms, and jargon. Want to write websites? It's easy enough to find out what SEO stands for—and you'll need to know!

News Delivered to Your In-Box

You can stay up-to-date on industry news with daily or weekly e-mail alerts by setting up a Google News Alert. From Google.com, click on "About Google" and select "Google Services and Tools" to find "Alerts." Type in specific phrases and words on what you'd like to see. For example, you may choose to see news items (and blog entries, discussions, and videos) on "property management." If you then find that you're seeing too many items that aren't relevant, you can refine your search criteria to "property management," "condominiums," and "Florida."

Get the Inside Scoop

If you feel you need some specific insights into the state of your chosen industry, try for one or more information interviews. These are one-on-one meetings that you set up with established professionals in your field. For more on information interviews, see chapter 8.

THE LAST WORD

The time you spend researching your chosen industry will pay off. It will help you set parameters for your job search now, and you can draw on the information you find when you're in an interview—to demonstrate your knowledge and insights in your field—as well as once you get a job. In fact, staying abreast of what's happening in your industry, including hiring trends, is always a good idea, even when you are employed. So make this type of research a habit!

Getting Down to Brass Tacks: The Ongoing Job Search

If you're unemployed and looking for a new job, your job search *is* your daily work. If you've got a job but are looking for another, you need to set time and energy aside each week for your job search, or you'll find you don't get very far. Here are some basic tips to help keep your search on track:

✦ **Be patient.** The length of time you look for a job before you get the perfect offer—or even the first phone interview—may be longer than you might expect. Depending on the state of the overall economy, the health of your industry, and just plain luck, you may have to spend many months on your search. That can be discouraging—especially when you don't hear back from many employers, or when you get multiple rejections—so steel yourself for the long haul.

✦ **Put in the hours.** Remember how you set a schedule at the beginning of your job search (chapter 1)? As your job search winds on, it's important to stick to that schedule. Do what it takes to put in the time you promised yourself, even if you have to break the time spent into two- or three-hour blocks.

✦ **Keep meeting your goals.** Your daily and weekly goals go hand in hand with your schedule. Keep striving for them, but if you find that the targets you originally set for yourself are unrealistic or too repetitive, it's OK to set new ones. Try to broaden your search without easing up on the amount of effort you put in.

✦ **Step away from the computer.** Remember—while the Internet is an amazing source for browsing job openings, career advice, and company research, there's more to a job search than Google. Make a point to get out of the house to volunteer and network formally and informally. You can start by heading over to your public library . . .

66 "Take advantage of the Internet. You have multiple ways of reaching companies. Of course, you certainly have to follow the directions for applying for an open position. But you can also follow up [through different channels] to differentiate yourself."
—Dionna Keels, a member of the SHRM (Society for Human Resource Management) staffing management expertise panel 99

Best in Show—Online Job Search

Bolles, Mark Emery, and Richard N. Bolles. *Job-Hunting Online: A Guide to Job Listings, Message Boards, Research Sites, the UnderWeb,*

Counseling, Networking, Self-Assessment Tools, Niche Sites. (Berkeley, CA: Ten Speed Press, 2008).

Dikel, Margaret Riley, and Frances E. Roehm. *Guide to Internet Job Searching, 2008–2009 ed.* (New York: McGraw-Hill, 2008).

Doyle, Alison. *Internet Your Way To a New Job: How to Really Find a Job Online.* (Cupertino, CA: Happy About, 2009).

Levinson, Jay Conrad, and David E. Perry. *Guerrilla Marketing for Job Hunters 2.0: 1,001 Unconventional Tips, Tricks and Tactics for Landing Your Dream Job.* (Hoboken, NJ: John Wiley & Sons, 2009).

Job-hunt, www.job-hunt.org.

The Riley Guide, "Sites with Job Listings," www.rileyguide.com/jobs.html.

Weddle's, www.weddles.com.

WetFeet, www.wetfeet.com.

Factoid

Where Recruiters and HR Professionals Plan to Post

WEDDLE's consulting firm surveyed 3,900 recruiters and HR professionals in 2005. Of those,

11 percent said they plan to use "general recruitment" websites.

84 percent said they preferred niche job boards.

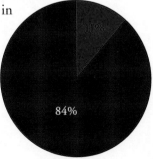

Factoid

Where Companies Say They Hire

CareerXroads' ninth Annual Source of Hire (SOH) study shows the following top five sources for hiring employees externally (that is, not promoting current employees):

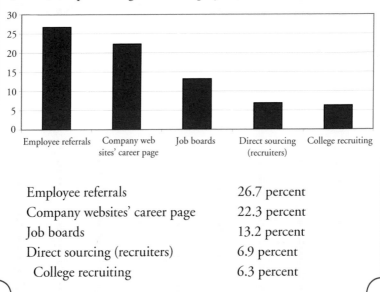

Employee referrals	26.7 percent
Company websites' career page	22.3 percent
Job boards	13.2 percent
Direct sourcing (recruiters)	6.9 percent
College recruiting	6.3 percent

WHERE TO LOOK ONLINE

CareerBuilder.com and Monster.com . . . industry-specific online forums and discussion groups . . . LinkedIn . . . about.com and career information sites . . . the Internet offers literally countless sites and pages that include job postings (such as local newspapers' online classified sections), career advice, and how-to descriptions for every aspect of job-seeking. The trick is to "search smart" and make your time online count.

HOW TO SEARCH

In order to find the best sites and the best individual listings, you have to choose your search words and phrases wisely. You can use the database resources listed in the "Sources for Keywords" section of chapter 4 to make a list of words to use in your Internet search.

"You have to find all the key terms that are going to deliver good search results," says Damone Virgilio, staff development manager at Memphis (Tennessee) Public Library. "Online searches are about sitting and combing through results. It can be tedious—but if you've been looking for a long time with no results, maybe a broader selection of results is better for you."

LIBRARY RESOURCES

Before you delve into hours of online research, check the website of your local public library. You might find that the experts there have already done some of the heavy lifting!

At Baltimore County (Maryland) Public Library, the Jobs and Info page gets about 1,000 hits a month. "People who know what they're looking for don't need the webpage, but those kind of new to job search will go online and find an overwhelming number of options, a mix of all kinds of sites that are rated by popularity rather than quality by the search engines," explains Jim DeArmey, the library's coordinator of information services. This webpage "takes one piece out of the process of the time-consuming and often overwhelming task of looking for a job."

DeArmey adds, "Our goal is to have a site that is manageably small. People visit because they're not the most practiced jobseekers." The library staff reviews the sites listed on their webpage regularly and adds anything they find useful, such as résumé how-tos and the library's Testing and Educational database.

Visit Baltimore County Public Library's Jobs and Info page at www.bcpl.info/info/jobs—then see what your own library system might offer online.

CHOOSE THE BEST JOB BOARDS

Your online job search should include regular visits to job boards—sites that display job postings. There are so many . . . how do you choose which sites to bookmark? Your list of regular boards might include:

+ **The big national sites** all allow you to post one or more version's of your résumé, so when you're ready to apply for a job you can do so quickly and easily.
+ **Your local newspaper's job listings**. Yes, some employers still advertise job openings in the newspaper—and those ads are typically found online.
+ **Industry-specific job boards** are a must for just about every job search. More efficient than wading through mismatches on the general national sites, and providing an at-a-glance overview of all opportunities within your profession. Simply plug appropriate words into your search engine to turn up sites for your career or industry, or try the Job Spider at www.thejobspider .com/job/directory/employment-resources.asp.
+ **Sites of professional associations.** Websites for most large associations now include job postings, and these can be even more targeted than industry job boards.
+ **Craigslist** for the city or region where you want to work. Yes, there are "real" jobs posted on Craigslist all the time—many

younger professionals consider Craigslist the go-to site for everything from selling furniture to buying event tickets, and that includes seeking job candidates. Plus, many employers love Craigslist because the ads are free!

✦ **Aggregators.** These sites can save you time and unearth more job postings than you might. They automatically draw job postings from numerous online sources large and small, including the major job boards and search firms, smaller niche sites, and corporate career sites. Damone Virgilio, staff development manager at Memphis (Tennessee) Public Library, prefers the aggregator Indeed.com. "It pulls job openings from different sites so it casts a wide net," he says. "It's also extremely easy to use; just enter your ZIP code and the job title."

JOB BOARD EXAMPLES

Big National Sites
www.CareerBuilder.com
www.monster.com

Industry-specific Job Boards
www.accounting.com
www.hrcareersusa.com (jobs in HR)
www.dice.com (careers in technology)

Professional Associations
Automotive Service Association: www.asashop.org
Marketing Research Association: www.mra-net.org
National Association of Veterinary Technicians: www.navta.net

Aggregators
www.indeed.com
www.simplyhired.com
www.topusajobs.com
www.linkup.com (aggregates only from company websites)

Job Boards Ranked

If you'd like some help from expert opinions and job-seeker statistics to help you determine the best (or most popular) job boards, check out these sources:

WEDDLE's User's Choice Awards (www.weddles.com/awards/index.htm), published each year, lists the winning general and specialty sites nominated by job-seekers and career activists.

The Classifieds News Blog posts an annual ranking of the top fifteen U.S. job-search websites at http://blog.daype.com/tips/top-us-job-search-websites.html.

Online Employment Testing

When applying for jobs online, you may come across an employer that requires you to take an online test as part of the application process. Preemployment tests or assessments are used as a first step to narrow the field of candidates. These tests may contain questions about your personality and work style, or they could check your hands-on skills at clerical tasks or work-related knowledge.

If you come across an opening that requires a test, make sure you are ready. Check that you are using a reliable Internet connection, have ample time, and—most important—understand what the open position entails and have some knowledge of the employing organization.

Be aware that some Internet applications enable employers to check how long it took you to complete the test, and see how you may have corrected or changed answers as you went.

LOG IN TO SEARCH EVERY DAY

Do your research: investigate all likely job boards, decide which are the best fit for you, check their privacy policies and security, and eliminate any aggregators that provide too many duplicates. (Note, too, that aggregators don't pull job listings from Craigslist.)

Bookmark all the boards you're interested in following, and visit each one often to check for new listings—if possible, do this every day. It doesn't take long to review only the latest listings, and you want to be able to respond to a job ad as soon as possible after it's posted: "I generally go through applicants chronologically, so it's good to be among the first to apply," says Dionna Keels, a member of the SHRM (Society for Human Resource Management) staffing management expertise panel. "That means you need to search for openings every day."

Many sites will send you regular updates with new listings via e-mail, but don't rely on these—you'll find many of the job mentions are off-target, because they are compiled by a software program.

Librarian's Top Pick

Virgilio says, "I love the extensive initial assessment you have to fill out on www.jobfox.com. You have to fill out a profile, which forces you to do some thinking about your skills and background—thinking that can be helpful to a job-seeker. One warning: you have to submit a résumé, and you'll get multiple e-mail solicitations from résumé specialists who want money to update your résumé for you."

COMPANY WEBSITES

You'd think that if an organization has a job opening, it would be posted on one or more of the job boards mentioned here. That is not always the case—so an organization's own website may be a gold mine of information. Part of your job-search time online should be spent researching likely employers, and when you find one, visit their website and look for "careers," "employment," "career opportunities," or a similar link to view open positions. You'll find a lot more detail here than in a paid ad—possibly the full job description, salary information, and more.

> "A lot of times, businesses will post jobs on their site first, before they go to the job boards."
>
> **—Barb Vlk, business librarian at Arlington Heights (Illinois) Public Library**

LINKEDIN JOB LISTINGS

LinkedIn has job listings, but the pickings are relatively slim compared to the types of sites listed above. However, time browsing on LinkedIn can definitely be well-spent: If you find a LinkedIn job posting you're interested in, you can apply using copy-and-paste sections from your plain-text résumé, as explained in chapter 4.

Each job posting will reveal whether you are "linked" to the posting company. On the right side of the page with the job description, you'll see any once-, twice- or three-times-removed connections. Click on one to see who you know that is connected. You'll also see whether you share any LinkedIn groups with the company's employees. Note that you have to view the actual job posting to see how you're connected to the hiring company.

If you see any connections to the company you're interested in working for, you can use LinkedIn to ask your connections for a referral (by clicking on the "Request Referral" button), which can greatly enhance your odds of standing out from other candidates for that job. You can also request an introduction to someone. If you want to contact a LinkedIn user who is two or three degrees away from you, you can request an introduction through one of your connections. Your connection will, in turn, decide whether to forward it on to the desired recipient (if in your "second-degree connections) or to a shared connection (if in your third-degree connections). You'll learn more about the networking power of LinkedIn in chapter 6.

Time Is Money

Be honest with how you're spending your time online. You may plan to spend two hours browsing job listings, but if you find that your search has led you through multiple sites until you're reading an article about how to dress for success, that's not productive.

In fact, the comprehensive job-search site Riley Guide (rileyguide. com) dictates, "Limit your time online to one-quarter (25%) of the total time you can dedicate to your job search."

BEWARE OF SCAMS

As you browse job listings, keep in mind that there are job scams out there. Don't answer any "employer" inquiries for personal information such as your Social Security number or bank account number—that goes for contact by phone, e-mail, on a website, or even in person.
Sharing this information is never part of the interviewing process.

And don't believe the job description that's too good to be true; if you could make $100,000 working from home, we'd all be doing it already!

WHERE TO LOOK OFF-LINE

Step away from the computer to find more opportunities to research, find, and apply for jobs. Remember that face-to-face networking is an important component to any job search (covered in chapter 6). Here is a look at other "off-line" resources and events to include in your search.

Job Fairs

Job fairs are hosted by colleges and universities, communities and profession-specific groups, or consortiums. Many job fairs are extremely general, with a wide range of employers and positions. Others  are targeted to specific industries or professions, such as a Technology Job Fair.

Finding a Fair

If you're plugged into the job-seekers' network, you'll automatically learn about upcoming job fairs through online forums and groups; they'll be advertised on career sites, and fellow members of your job support group or networking circle will tell you. You may also find out through local newspapers, bulletin boards, and your local unemployment office.

Preparing for a Fair

It's important to do your legwork in advance of showing up at a job fair. This includes more than just preregistering and ironing your best shirt:

1. Find out which prospective employers will be participating, and select which you want to be sure to meet. Take time to do some online research to check out each one before the fair.
2. If a map of the fair is available, literally plan your route.
3. Know what you want from this particular fair, and have an appropriate elevator speech prepared. (For an explanation of elevator speeches, see chapter 6.)
4. Have plenty of copies of appropriate résumés and business cards ready.
5. If you have a portfolio, prepare that as well.
6. Rehearse your elevator speech and practice answering interview questions.
7. Select the business attire you plan to wear, clean and prepare it, and try it on to make sure everything is ready.
8. Have a professional-looking briefcase ready to hold résumés and portfolio, and use it to carry the materials you gather at the fair.

Working the Fair

If possible, get to the job fair early, get through registration, and start working your map route by visiting your list of "top picks" first. (Don't forget to check at registration to see if there are any last-minute additions of hiring companies.) At each table or booth you visit, try these strategies:

+ Pick up the handouts they provide, and review them if possible before engaging in conversation.
+ When you're ready to talk—or when the recruiter makes eye contact—greet them and give a firm handshake along with your elevator speech. Keep in mind that the employees working the job fair are probably not the hiring managers; they are HR professionals who are screeners for the company.

- ✦ Take notes during each conversation or interview so you'll be able to keep them straight when you get home.
- ✦ Make sure you get business cards or contact information for everyone you might want to follow up with—and give them yours.
- ✦ Take advantage of the pool of job-seekers, and network with them as well. Find out what's working best for them.

After the Fair

When you get home from the job fair, organize the business cards and information you collected. Input all relevant details into your job-search organization system. And be sure to write thank-you e-mails or notes to each recruiter you talked to—and send those thank-yous within a day or two.

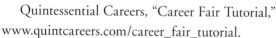

Best in Show—Job Fairs

CollegeGrad.com, "Job Fair Success," www .collegegrad.com/jobsearch/Job-Fair-Success.

Quintessential Careers, "Career Fair Tutorial," www.quintcareers.com/career_fair_tutorial.

Publications

The printed page still plays a role in your job search. Browse these sources—at least some of which may be found for free at your local library—to look for job openings, keep

up with industry and business news, and find key players you might contact for an information interview or even a job interview:

+ Your local newspapers
+ Industry trade journals (*Midwest Engineer, Journal of Hospitality Financial Management*)
+ Association newsletters and magazines (*Professional Photographer* magazine, *Interior Design in Practice*)
+ Your college's alumni newsletter or magazine

Government and Nonprofit Agencies

Every community has public and private agencies that serve job-seekers. Ask the reference librarian at your public library about resources (and job listings) offered by your local unemployment office, state and local government agencies, and nonprofit offices. You might get advice from these groups on interviewing, résumés, and much more. And  each will have compiled sources of job listings that may be new to you. Look for agencies such as:

Maryland's Office of Workforce Development
Cincinnati's SuperJobs, a nonprofit center for job-seekers
The Nashville Career Advancement Center
Michigan Works

Recruitment and Temp Agencies

Signing up for temporary work is a great way to look for a job. Many companies will hire a temporary worker who has proven herself on the job, despite an often-hefty fee they must pay to the temp agency. Even if a temp assignment doesn't lead to a permanent job, you'll find it has other benefits:

1. Working at a company for a day, week, or many months will help you clarify your employment goals. What type of corporate culture do you prefer? What type of boss do you work well with?

2. You'll pick up new skills with every assignment, whether it's mastering a telephone system or getting training in specialty software.

3. You can broaden your network with every assignment. Connect with your coworkers and let them know you'd like to find work in their industry.

4. Temp agencies often do general recruiting as well. You can prove yourself with an agency—especially if you didn't sign on with a strong background—and increase your chances of landing an interview for a permanent job.

5. At the end of a long-term temp assignment, ask your direct manager for a letter of recommendation. This can help fill a large unemployment gap if you've been job-seeking for many months.

What Recruiters Say

Two professional recruiters reveal how they search for the best candidates . . .

Jill Silman, SPHR, vice president at Meador Staffing Services and a spokesperson for the Society of Human Resources Management (SHRM):

"Our number one method has always been referrals. But we're finding that social media is becoming more effective and efficient. That's quickly becoming number two: as individual recruiters and as an organization, we'll use Facebook, LinkedIn, and Twitter to look for candidates."

***

Dionna Keels, a member of the SHRM (Society for Human Resource Management) staffing management expertise panel:

"I've been in recruiting for about ten years. Over the past four to five years, online resources have been huge for me. The big online boards are a really good tool. I'll search the online résumé banks by skills, job titles, and even by company.

"I use the big job boards—Careerbuilder and Monster—but I definitely use more specific ones also. Dice is a good one for IT positions. I also look at association job boards. Being involved in an [industry-related] association is a great way to look for a job.

"How do you stand out in a group of 500 résumés? Well, if you're applying for a position that looks like a perfect match for your skills and experience, you can also do some research on, say, LinkedIn, and maybe shoot a separate e-mail to HR or the hiring manager to highlight yourself. In one case where I had 500 résumés to look at, I got separate e-mails from ten or fifteen people. I was more likely to look harder at those résumés."

STAY ORGANIZED FROM THE START

As you begin your job search, keep track of everything. You'll be glad you did—especially when you get a call from a company you don't remember applying to, or meet someone for the second time at a networking event.

You'll need to devise a system that keeps track of details on all jobs you apply for—at every stage, your networking contacts, and your prospects for hiring companies. You'll want to note *at least* the following information:

Jobs applied for

+ Where you found the job posting—list the specific job board or publication

- The job title and any identifier code
- The company name and address if available
- Contact names and titles, with phone number or e-mails
- The date and time you applied or responded
- Which version of your résumé and cover letter were sent or used to complete the application

If you interviewed, add:

- The names and titles of everyone you spoke with
- The date and time of your interview
- Notes you might need to refer to for a follow-up interview
- What follow-up you took and when—thank-you notes sent, phone calls, etc.

Here is an example of what your "jobs applied for" tracking might look like:

Date	Ad source	Position	Company	Contact
11/3/10	Omaha job board	Sales associate	unknown	unknown
11/5/10	careerbuilder	Regional sales representative	Meteor Marketing	Sally Cottering, HR
11/5/10	careerbuilder	Assistant manager, sales	Premium Coffee Co.	unknown
11/7/10	Omaha sales meet-up	Sales associate	GreensJeans Co.	Bertram Green

In a different area, record your networking contacts. For these, include:

+ Which event—or where or when you met the person
+ The name, business title, and company of each individual, along with contact information
+ Notes to help you remember them
+ What follow-up you took and when e-mail sent, information interview requested, etc.

If a networking contact becomes a "job applied for," simply copy the information to your other tracking sheet.

You can record your entries on paper if you prefer—dedicate a notebook or file to your job hunt—but using computer software like Microsoft Excel will be better. That's because you will be able to search on a company name, sort your search chronologically or alphabetically by any field, and easily add or revise information.

Address/phone	Website	Résumé/ application	Result	Follow-up
unknown	unknown	Sales11.1.doc		
cotterling@ meteormarketing. com	*www. meteormarketing. com*	Sales.11.5.txt		
unknown	*www. goodcoffeesales. com*	Salesmgmt. 10.15.doc		
1444 W. Grand Ave., Omaha Ste. 322	*www.greensjeans. com*	Sales11.1.doc	phone interview scheduled 11/20/10	

Here is an example of what your "networking" tracking might look like:

Date	Event/network	Name	Company
11/7/10	Omaha sales meet-up	Bertram Green	GreensJeans Co.
11/7/10	Omaha sales meet-up	Joe Carlson	Carlson Recruiting
11/7/10	Omaha sales meet-up	Wendy Maris	GBV Partners
11/15/10	Library job group	Sandra Anders, Regional sales	ABC Corporation
11/15/10	Library job group	Sarah Jones, Director of Sales	Meteor Marketing
11/15/10	NSWA Nov. meeting	Fred Fredericks, Sales manager	Premium Coffee Co.

Address/phone	Website	Follow-up	Result
1444 W. Grand Ave., Omaha Ste. 322	*www.greensjeans.com*	sent e-mail 11/9/10	phone interview scheduled 11/20/10
4422 W. Grand Ave., Omaha	*www.carlsonplaces.com*	sent résumé 11/9/10	interview 11/15/10
3321 Yarrow St., Omaha	*www.gbvpinc.com*	sent résumé 11/9/10	
832 SW 124th Place, Omaha	unknown	Send article on Google marketing	
9324 Great Neck Drive, Omaha	*www.meteormarketing.com*	none	
693 W. Grand Ave., Omaha	*www.goodcoffeesales.com*	requested info interview 11/16/10	Call back after holiday

Why Stay Organized?

Primarily, your tracking system will help you remember when and where you applied for jobs, and possibly connect some very important dots: When you realize that the person you met at a fund-raiser last week works at a company that just posted a promising job, for example. But it can also help you in other ways:

+ Use your tracking system(s) to set and check your job-hunting goals. For example, you may decide that you must attend at least one networking event every week, and collect at least five relevant business cards at each. Your tracking sheet will hold you accountable!
+ By logging where you're finding job openings and which ones have netted you results (a phone interview, for example), you

can see at a glance which resources are the best. When you take a little time to look at all the data you've collected over a month, you may see that while the majority of jobs you applied to all came from one major online job board, the two interviews you had were for openings you found through a professional networking group.

✦ Your list of networking contacts may come in handy throughout your career. Save it, update it, and keep adding to it even after you land your perfect job. These people may be resources for future projects or future employers—or future employees, when you're ready to hire someone in your own department!

Free Online Resource

Before you set up your perfect tracking system, check out Jibber-Jobber. This is a free online service that provides all sorts of tracking functions, including tracking expenses for your job hunt, interview prep, a calendar, and a contact management function. Basic membership is free, but the premium package will cost you. It's definitely worth a look: http://jobhunt.jibberjobber.com/index.php.

THE LAST WORD

Be prepared to remain ignorant. That's because many hiring companies simply don't contact job applications who don't make the cut. Some don't even contact those who make it to the interview stage to let them know "thanks, but no thanks." You'll send out many résumés, fill out many applications, and shake many hands with absolutely no idea what happened. . . . The only thing you can do is follow up if possible, and bide your time. Keep your records of jobs applied for, in case the Silent Company does indeed contact you down the road.

Writing Résumés Right

Your résumé holds the most prominent place in your job search. It acts as your foot in the door and your handshake; it summarizes your experience and unique qualifications, and is pretty much the single most common step (if not hurdle) in gaining any interview.

While opinions vary on how résumés are used by employers, what they should look like, and the information they should contain, you have to have one—and it should be the best résumé you can manage to create!

> "Your résumé is your opportunity to make a first impression."
>
> **—Jill Silman, SPHR, vice president at Meador Staffing Services and a spokesperson for the Society of Human Resources Management (SHRM)**

7 WAYS YOU'LL USE YOUR RÉSUMÉ

1. As part of networking. In a one-on-one follow-up meeting or at an information interview, ask your new contact to critique your résumé and your experience. This is an acceptable, discreet way to see if your experience and qualifications are in line with the type of position you're looking for.

2. In response to an advertised job opening. Most employers request a copy of your résumé as the very first step in choosing a candidate.

3. As an introduction when no job opening has been advertised. E-mail or hand your résumé to a hiring manager.

4. As the basis for your profile on LinkedIn or for online job applications.

5. Keep a copy handy to refer to for phone interviews and conversation points during networking events.

6. Bring multiple copies to job fairs that you attend.

7. Have at least one copy with you for all in-person interviews.

Best in Show—Résumés

Dikel, Margaret, and Frances Roehm. *The Guide to Internet Job Searching.* (New York: McGraw-Hill, 2008).

McGraw-Hill's Big Red Book of Resumes (New York: McGraw-Hill, 2002).

Ireland, Susan. *The Complete Idiot's Guide to the Perfect Resume.* (New York: Alpha Books, 2010).

Whitcomb, Susan Britton. *Résumé Magic.* (JIST Works, Inc., 1999).

Whitcomb, Susan Britton, and Pat Kendall. *e-Resumes: Everything You Need to Know about Using Electronic Resumes to Tap into Today's Job Market.* (New York: McGraw-Hill, 2002).

The Riley Guide, http://rileyguide.com/resprep.html.

The Damn Good Resume website, www.damngood.com.

Dummies.com, "Resumes," www.dummies.com/how-to/business-careers/careers/Resumes.html.

RÉSUMÉ-WRITING 101

Chronological vs. Functional Résumés

There are two main formats for résumés. The chronological résumé is the most common, listing your work history in order with your most recent job first. The other format is the functional résumé, which contains the same general information and categories as the chronological résumé, only reorganized to highlight your strengths—  typically in order to downplay your work history (or lack thereof).

The functional résumé is best used when:

+ You are changing careers and your work history doesn't apply very well to your desired position.
+ You are a recent graduate, or have limited work experience.
+ You have long gaps in employment, a widely varied work history, or other work-history issues that may be glaringly obvious in a chronological résumé.

You can begin your functional résumé with a section on "Accomplishments" or "Achievements," where you list three to five skill areas. If possible, use career skills (such as bookkeeping, computer repair, or project management) instead of personal ones (attention to detail, technically savvy, organized). Each accomplishment or skill can be described succinctly. Note that you still need to include a work history section within your functional résumé, but it can be a basic listing of job title, employer, and length of employment.

FOR INSTANCE . . .

The job-seeker who just lost his job as regional sales manager of a well-known company is going to highlight his work history—particularly that last job. The newly minted college grad is going to highlight her new information technology degree, her student activities and honors in college, etc.—before listing her history of part-time retail jobs.

Regardless of format, all résumés should include

+ A letterhead-like heading that includes your name, one phone number and one e-mail address where you can be reached, and possibly your mailing address
+ Some work history, no matter how brief or relevant
+ Education history (at minimum, schools attended and degrees or certifications earned—or classwork completed)

Your résumé *may* include

+ A career objective or similar statement about what type of position you're seeking
+ Keywords section (see below)
+ Educational honors, extracurricular activities
+ Volunteer work and experience
+ Professional honors
+ List of professional memberships
+ Special skills, software or computer systems mastered, typing speed, etc.

> "I don't think everyone has to follow 'hard and fast' résumé rules—it's all relative to the person and their situation."
>
> **—Damone Virgilio, staff development manager at Memphis (Tennessee) Public Library**

LIBRARY RESOURCES

When you're ready to write or revise your résumé, head straight to your public library to find out what resources they can offer. Ask a reference or business librarian what the library has. In addition to books and possibly Internet-based resources, you may find in-library workshops or classes on résumé-writing, or one-on-one résumé review from a librarian or volunteer.

RÉSUMÉ Q&A

Q: I have a lot of work history. How long can my résumé be?

A: "It depends on the person, the experience, and the job," says Damone Virgilio, staff development manager at Memphis (Tennessee) Public Library. "If there is a lot of experience, you may get into two pages. But my theory is that if you're going to two pages, use *all* of those pages. If you end up with a page and quarter, you need to edit back to a single page." If your résumé is two pages long, keep the most important information on the first page, and make sure the second page includes your name.

Q: Is that true for my *electronic* résumé?

A: When sending your résumé in the body of an e-mail or copying its content into an online form, the rule is to "write tight." Shorten all sections of text to keep everything as brief as possible. You can bring a printout of the full version of your résumé along to your first interview!

Q: Do I have to list every single job?

A: Not necessarily. If experience is not relevant to the job(s) you're applying for, you can leave it out—unless that will leave a suspicious gap in your work history. Space on your résumé is valuable, so don't waste it on a job that doesn't translate to what you're looking for now.

Q: How should I handle gaps in my employment?

A: "If a person lacks education, has gaps in their work history or a number of jobs of very short duration, that doesn't look good," says Virgilio. "In these cases, you may focus on the skills you've acquired throughout their career. You still have to list past jobs with dates, but if you pack the front of the résumé with your core competencies and with measurable evidence of achievement, you switch the focus to what you can do."

Q: I've never worked before. What should I put in my résumé?

A: This is a perfect situation to use a functional résumé format rather than a chronological one. Put the focus on your strengths, knowledge, and intelligence. Start with a statement of what you can offer the hiring company, and include the following, if applicable:

✦ Volunteer work. Don't have any? Get some immediately—preferably something related to your field.

+ Work experience. Briefly mention any work experience at all, to show you know how to be responsible and earn a paycheck.
+ Intenships. New graduates should definitely highlight any they have worked.
+ Extracurricular activities, including sports.

THE SKINNY ON CVS

What if a job posting requires a CV? Typically used for academic or research positions, educational administration jobs, or admission to graduate school, a curriculum vitae—CV for short—is Latin for "the course of (one's) life." A CV includes much more detail than a résumé, and outlines your academic and professional accomplishments.

For more on CVs, visit www.career.vt.edu/JOBSEARC/Resumes/vitae.htm.

KEYWORDS

The Key to Employers Finding You

Later in this chapter you'll learn about creating multiple versions of your résumé—but all versions should include the most crucial component of any job search: keywords.

When your résumé is received by a potential employer, it will be scanned—either by a human or a software program—for keywords. If your résumé doesn't include enough keywords, or the right keywords, it won't even make the first cut.

FOR INSTANCE . . .

You're applying for a position as a payroll clerk. Your résumé might be scanned for the following words and phrases:

+ Payroll
+ Timekeeping
+ Payroll discrepancies
+ Verify
+ Exemptions
+ Earnings and deductions
+ Compile
+ Analyze
+ Names of software programs or degrees specified in the job posting

One way to ensure the appropriate keywords end up in every version of your résumé is to include a specific section just for this purpose. In *Job-Hunting Online,* 5th ed., Mark Emery Bolles and Richard Nelson Bolles state, " . . . it has become standard practice to place a line or two at the end of a résumé intended for online submission, headed by the term 'Keywords:' and followed by a series of words, separated by commas, that are designed solely to trigger the search engine when an employer enters his search terms."

Part of Virgilio's job is to help Memphis Public Library patrons create and revise their résumés. He says, "I'll generally insert a table at the top of the résumé and put bullet points of core competencies. This is similar to a keyword section."

If you're changing careers, or looking for your first job in your chosen profession, load keywords into a section on "career goals" or "career objective" so that your résumé will survive the scan.

> "Keywords are vital if job seekers are to be found in an online database. . . . Without a doubt, a résumé posted at a career site such as Monster.com will be warehoused in a searchable database. Here, paid subscribers search résumés using keywords . . . the right keywords will determine whether your résumé is 'lost' or 'found.'"
>
> **—Susan Britton Whitcomb and Pat Kendall in *e-Resumes: Everything You Need to Know about Using Electronic Resumes to Tap into Today's Job Market***

SOURCES FOR KEYWORDS

How do you find keywords? Virgilio states, "You definitely want to look at the job posting, and get a hold of the job description if you can—that's fantastic. Look at the words used and focus on including those words. Also, look at the industry and use the jargon and terms that employers will look for and recognize."

Another great keywords source is databases available online for free or through your public library's website: "Databases are very good for finding keywords," says Barb Vlk, business librarian at Arlington Heights (Illinois) Public Library. "The best is the *Occupational Outlook Handbook,* published as a free website and in print by the Bureau of Labor Statistics. It's got lots of information under each occupation. Everything there will give you keywords you can use in your résumé."

Vlk's advice is, "Start making a list of keywords from all these resources. Then beef up your résumé every time you apply for a job."

Best in Show—Databases

"A lot of people come in looking for help with their résumé-writing skills. Our databases offer great templates and tools that they can use," says Jerome L. Myers, MLS, main library manager at the Tacoma (Washington) Public Library's Education and Job Center.

1. Myers' current favorite database for job-seekers is **JobNow,** which offers services that are free to library patrons. (The library pays a hefty subscription fee.) "JobNow lets you submit your résumé for review by a résumé specialist—you get their suggestions back within twenty-four hours," says Myers. "You can also chat live with someone through JobNow to practice your interview skills. Log in between one and five in the afternoon, and you can have a trial interview. They'll type in an interview question and you respond with your answer, then they critique it and tell you what you should and shouldn't have said."

2. "The **Testing and Education Center** database from Gale has a feature where you can store your résumé as a PDF. Most people bring a flash drive" so they can carry their résumés home or use them on different computers, says Myers.

3. "**The Job and Career Accelerator** has a component where you can research careers. It also includes job listings for a real job search."

Myers explains, "Some databases are more user-friendly than others. Some are easier to use, and might seem too basic to some users."

READY TO WRITE?

For many people, getting started on writing or revising their résumé is the toughest part. Follow these steps to get past "résumé-writer's block":

1. Look at sample résumés to get ideas. Check out books on résumé-writing from your library, or look at samples online. One site to visit is http://wetfeet.com/Experienced-Hire/Resume—Cover-letter.aspx.

2. Dump all information for your work history and education into a word-processing document. Double-check the dates, titles, and details of each job position; make sure your education, grade point average, or other information is included; then save that document.

3. Write to your audience. How can your experience, skills, and degrees benefit *them?* How will your work history translate to learning a new job?

4. Next, outline the information and add sections as preferred: keywords, summary statement, etc.

5. Go back and edit. Tighten up the writing to keep it concise and action-oriented (lots of verbs), and include focus on specific accomplishments or responsibilities. You don't have to use complete sentences; bulleted lists of statements are best.

6. Once you feel you have a complete draft, format the document so that it's visually appealing. (See "Your Hard-Copy Résumé" below.)

7. Proofread the final document twice, then once reading backward.

8. Ask at least one other person to review it and proofread it again.

9. Save your final document and prepare to rewrite a version for each job you apply for.

"People will hire you for one of two reasons: because they want to make money or they want to save money. So anything you can say in your résumé to show you've done that in the past is guaranteed to get you noticed. Use specific numbers, percentages, budget responsibility, etc. to demonstrate what you've done."
—Jill Silman, SPHR, vice president at Meador Staffing Services and a spokesperson for the Society of Human Resources Management (SHRM)

FORMATTED AND PLAIN-TEXT RÉSUMÉS

Today's job-seeker will most likely be submitting résumés via e-mail or websites. So you'll need your beautifully formatted word-processing document to use for a hard-copy résumé, but you'll also need to be ready to have an electronic and plain-text version as well, so you can quickly submit your résumé according to the job posting's requirements. Here's an overview of these résumé formats.

"The truth of the matter is that the way we're submitting résumés has changed—it's all electronic now—but the process is basically the same."
—Damone Virgilio, staff development manager at Memphis (Tennessee) Public Library

YOUR FORMATTED RÉSUMÉ

So you've written a solid draft of your résumé in a word-processing program such as Microsoft Word. What should it look like?

RÉSUMÉ FORMATTING DOS AND DON'TS

DO start with your biggest selling point. "I like to recommend a section at the beginning of the résumé that stands out, something that brings out the best that the person can bring to the table," says Virgilio. "It could be a list of skills, certifications, or software mastered. You have to emphasize what separates you from the pack."

DON'T cram in as many words as possible to fill up the page. This makes it uninviting to read or even skim. "Someone who's looking through 150 résumés is looking for a reason to eliminate as many as possible," Virgilio points out. "If a résumé is not easy to read, they're going to throw it out." He recommends using a 12-point font with at least the standard space between lines.

DO edit every job description down to the most salient points. "One of the biggest problems I see with résumés that people bring in is formatting," says Virgilio. "I see lots of text on a page with way too much description of duties, so nothing jumps out."

DON'T forget to proofread! A résumé with a typo will end up in the trashcan. "My advice is as basic as please, please, please proofread anything before you send it," says Jill Silman, SPHR, vice president at Meador Staffing Services and a spokesperson for the Society of Human Resources Management (SHRM). "Use the old trick of reading something backwards to make sure your mind doesn't jump ahead."

DO print out the résumé on good-quality white (or off-white) paper. Always have a crisp, clean copy or two ready at an in-person interview.

Once you have your résumé final and looking good, you can print it out and use as hard copies, or send it as an e-mail attachment—either as a Microsoft Word or PDF document. If you use a word-processing program other than Word, you should save it as a file type that anyone can open—and these days, that includes Word files. Other options are PDFs or Rich Text Files.

A Case for Sending PDFs

"We always have people do a Word document, then tell the person they can save it as a PDF and e-mail it," reports Virgilio. "A PDF can't be inadvertently changed by someone else, and any computer can read it—you don't have to worry about software versions. It also shows a bit of tech savvy on the sender's part—you know how to make a PDF."

If you don't have Adobe PDF Writer, you can download free software that allows you to easily convert a document into a PDF. PDFCreator is available at http://sourceforge.net/projects/pdfcreator. (For Windows systems only.)

YOUR PLAIN-TEXT RÉSUMÉ

In addition to your carefully formatted résumé, you'll want a plain-text version as well—one that has all formatting and special characters stripped out. You will use this to copy and paste into the body of an e-mail (see "send two in one" below) or to copy and paste sections into an online application form. Some employers may even request that you send in this version, if they are using certain software to scan all submitted résumés.

Turn Your Résumé into a Job Application

Many of the general job boards (including CareerBuilder.com and Monster.com) include an online application for any position; this is where you'll copy and paste your plain-text résumé into appropriate fields. The employer will never see your actual résumé—until you hand it over at your first in-person interview.

Here are five tips for turning your résumé into a plain-text document:

1. Strip out all formatting, including bold, italics, centering. Use one typeface and size—preferably something commonly used like Times or Arial.
2. Change formatting to remove columns or tabbed sections.
3. Remove bullet points.
4. Remove hard returns at the end of lines.
5. Save your document as a text file with the extension .txt to ensure all invisible coding is stripped out.
6. Review the plain-text document using a text editor program such as Notepad or SimpleText to ensure you're seeing it accurately.

ASC What?

A plain-text document may also be called an ASCII file—pronounced ASK-ee. ASCII is short for American Standard Code of Information Interchange. Saving a document as a text file and stripping out all coding and special characters (characters that use keyboard commands such as accented e's or em dashes) is basically the same thing as creating an ASCII file.

SENDING RÉSUMÉS BY E-MAIL

When you respond to a job posting—especially an online posting—you will more than likely be submitting your résumé electronically. But what exactly does that mean? Here is a handy checklist of points to consider.

1. Meet their requirements. Double-check any details on *what* the employer requires from applicants and *how* they wish to receive it. If possible, check the employer's company website for information on preferred method.

NOTE: If a job posting simply says "e-mail your résumé . . ." then it's safest to send your résumé as plain text (see below) within the body of your e-mail—with no attachment.

If the employer requests an attached file for the résumé, do they specify what file type? They may want résumés only submitted as Microsoft Word documents, or PDFs, or plain-text files, depending on their screening procedures.

2. Don't get blocked! With today's sophisticated spam filters, many company e-mail servers will block all attachments from certain types of e-mail addresses—or they may block only certain types of attachments such as Zip files or PDFs.

3. Send two in one. If an employer requests your résumé as a Word document, PDF, or other attachment, your best bet is to attach your résumé as requested, but also copy and paste the plain-text version of your résumé into the body of the e-mail. That way, if your attachment is not received, your résumé will still be in their hands.

4. Choose your subject line carefully. The subject line—the text that appears in the receiver's in-box—should make it clear what your e-mail is in response to, and perhaps sell you a little too. If responding to a specific job opening, use the job title or code used in the posting. If you're sending your résumé unsolicited, make the subject line a descriptor of you: "Database manager with 12 years experience" or "Physical therapist seeks challenging opportunity."

5. Be savvy about attachment names. If you're sending your résumé as an attachment, make sure you name it so that it's easily identifiable. Yourlastname_résumé.doc is your best bet—and be sure to include the extension .doc or .pdf so that it can be opened easily!

CUSTOMIZE YOUR RÉSUMÉ

"These days, you create a master résumé, and then every time you apply for a job you have to save it and tweak it for that specific job."

—Barb Vlk, business librarian at Arlington Heights (Illinois) Public Library

You'll never finish writing your résumé.

That's because every time you apply for a posted job opening, you should review your original résumé, save it as a new document, and then revise to best match the advertised opening. This might include changing or adding keywords, shifting emphasis within your work history, tweaking your summary statement, or all of the above.

Keep all versions of your résumé so that you can refer to which document you sent to which employer—and so that you have multiple versions to fine-tune for future applications. This is true for both your formatted résumés and your plain-text résumés.

Why do you need to keep all those résumés? Let's say you e-mailed a résumé to apply for a job two weeks ago, and now you need a print copy for your first interview. Which version did you send? You'd better find out, so that all copies of your résumé match exactly!

That's why you need to include your résumé version in your job-search tracking system.

If you do your job-searching and résumé-writing from more than one computer—or if you want to take information to your public library to revise or apply—consider keeping all your résumés on a flash drive, so you can update, revise, and send from another computer if necessary.

One last word on creating multiple versions of your résumé: Be sure to thoroughly proofread all new versions before you send them out!!

POSTING YOUR RÉSUMÉ ONLINE

Many job boards and career-oriented sites allow you to post a version (or more) of your résumé so that hiring companies and recruiters can find you. This is typically done by filling out an online form (copying and pasting from your best plain-text version).

Keep It Contained

While it may seem like a great idea to post your résumé everywhere you possibly can in order to get the most exposure, consider this: It's a better idea to maintain control of your own information. Don't allow a site to "blast" your résumé to various places, and don't fill out a profile that contains all your personal contact information. This will protect you from e-mail spam, unwanted contacts, and even identity theft!

Consider this strategy instead: definitely post one or more versions of your résumé on CareerBuilder.com and/or monster.com, as well as a couple of more specialized job sites for your industry or region. But before you choose those smaller sites, read their privacy policies to see if they can sell or share your information.

Keep It Private

If you're discreetly looking for a new job while still employed, keep in mind that your posted résumés may be found by coworkers and supervisors at your current employer. If you want to keep your job search on the down low, you can remove employer company names and replace with

Position applied for	Company	Résumé used	Date sent
Sales associate	GoodJeans Co.	Sales11.1.doc	11/3/10
Regional sales representative	Meteor Marketing	Sales.11.5.txt	11/5/10
Assistant manager, sales	Premium Coffee Co.	Salesmgmt.10.15.doc	11/5/10

descriptors. If your current employer is Advanced Computer Systems and you don't want to be found by a search on that name, replace with "mid-sized technology consulting company."

Keep It Fresh

It's true for the large job sites and may be for some smaller sites as well: when you revise and update your résumé, it moves back to the top of the list in associated databases. So try to add or change something every month or so to "refresh" your standings.

Creating Your Own Résumé Site

Another way to share your résumé with potential employers is to post it on your own website, or simply create a one-page site that is your résumé.

An added bonus for those job-seekers that show portfolios of their work, such as graphic designers or architects: you can post samples on the same site.

Pros and Cons

Pros

1. A web-based résumé is easy to share during networking, telephone interviews, and other meetings—just tell the other person the URL where it can be found.
2. Employers and recruiters may find you first, if they are searching the web for candidates with keywords.
3. An online résumé can include live links to your work samples, previous employers' websites, etc.

Cons

1. You'll need to purchase or find space on a web server to host your résumé—and hire someone to create an HTML page from your current résumé, or learn how to do it yourself.

2. If you're currently employed and your employer doesn't know you're looking for a new job, your résumé may pop up during a Google search.

3. Forget about the various versions of your résumé—you should post only one, which might end up being too limiting.

If you're a university student or recent grad, check with your school to see if provides web space for graduates.

One last word: **Don't** use your personal or family website to hold your résumé. Pictures of your grandchildren—or of you cavorting at a wedding—are not to be associated with your search. If you decide to post your résumé online, keep it separate!

WHAT HIRERS SAY

As you're sending out dozens of résumés, answering online job ads every day, and cold-calling local companies, do you ever wonder what the people at the other end of your job search are thinking? Here are a few "inside tips" from professionals who read résumés like yours every day:

Jill Silman, SPHR, vice president at Meador Staffing Services and a spokesperson for the Society of Human Resources Management (SHRM), says that her recruiting company receives résumés by e-mail (as attachments) or uploaded to their website. Therefore, "The more plainly they're formatted, the better. We prefer [Word documents] so that if we need to reformat it for a client, we can." She encourages job-seekers to also check the format of their résumé for consistency: "If you put one employer name in boldface, use boldface for all of them."

Her company keeps résumés in a database, and searches on keywords for each specific opening. "We get some résumés that have a keywords section, and that's fine—I don't have a problem with that. We do see some where the person has been counseled to put keywords in small, white type at the bottom of the résumé so they're invisible; the problem with that is that if the words aren't used in the body of the résumé, when the recruiter goes to look at the résumé, they can't see the words."

***

Dionna Keels, a member of the SHRM (Society for Human Resource Management) staffing management expertise panel, says, "I definitely prefer a Word document that's nicely formatted. Your formatting is really important. A résumé that's formatted well is more appealing to the eye and it's easier to read."

She adds, "What's important now is that people are able to point out specific things they've accomplished rather than a laundry list of job duties. Include measurable accomplishments, such as "'I saved x amount of dollars by improving a process.'"

And if your work history includes gaps or multiple short stays at jobs, Keels recommends, "Consider including a footnote about why you left. That way you're not leaving it up to the recruiter's imagination." Another option is to address the issue in your cover letter.

THE LAST WORD

The job-seeker who has been on the market for a while will end up with many, many different versions of her résumé. Be precise in naming each document, use electronic folders for different categories, and periodically refresh your memory as to which jobs you've applied for. That way, when you come across an open position you want to apply for, you can quickly decide which résumé version to work off of, find that document and revise to fit the opening, and you're good to go. Just remember to save and file the new résumé as well!

Crafting Effective Cover Letters

As with résumés, just about every job-search expert seems to have a different opinion on the worth of cover letters. But we're here to tell you: cover letters matter. A good one can enhance your résumé. A great one can move it to the top of the stack. A lousy one . . . well, you get the picture.

> "We don't see many cover letters anymore, but they are very important. The letter is your opportunity to really sell yourself."
>
> **—Jill Silman, SPHR, vice president at Meador Staffing Services and a spokesperson for the Society of Human Resources Management (SHRM)**

COVER ALL BASES

A cover letter serves multiple purposes. Traditionally, it has served as a formal introduction, but a savvy job-seeker can use it to do so much more. For example: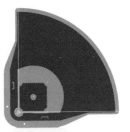

+ You can show off your knowledge of the company or industry that you learned thorough research.
+ You can highlight a specific skill or experience you have that's a great match for this opening.
+ You can explain—briefly and with a positive spin—any possible red flags in your résumé, such as a long gap in employment or multiple short-term jobs.
+ You can demonstrate your sharp communication skills and business writing abilities with a well-crafted letter.
+ You can let your personality peek through a little. Show some enthusiasm and verve in describing how much you want the position!

What Recruiters Say

Not all recruiters are sold on cover letters. Dionna Keels, a member of the SHRM (Society for Human Resource Management) staffing management expertise panel, calls them "a matter of personal preference" on the part of recruiters or HR professionals. "I don't put a lot of weight on them; however, if I'm trying to narrow down a small group of good candidates, the letter might become a deciding factor," she says.

Keels warns: "However, cover letters are another place where people have misspellings and bad sentence structure."

CUSTOMIZE EACH COVER

Always write a fresh cover letter to match the job you're applying for. It's even more important to customize the cover letter than the résumé. That's because you use the letter to pinpoint why you are perfect for this particular job. Study the job description or posted ad carefully, and make sure you address every point mentioned.

And be sure to save all your cover letter versions just as you do your résumés; you'll want to pull phrases and sentences from previous letters to build current ones. It's not as important to keep track of cover letters after you send them, but your letter may come in handy as a reminder of the key skills or accomplishments you spelled out for a particular job.

Finally, remember to proofread every single version of your cover letter before you send it. A single typo or misspelled word spells R-E-J-E-C-T-I-O-N.

Best in Show—Cover Letters

Betrus, Michael. *202 Great Cover Letters.* (New York: McGraw-Hill, 2008).

Enelow, Wendy, and Louise Kursmark. *Cover Letter Magic.* (Indianapolis, IN: JIST Works, 2010).

Yate, Martin. *Knock 'em Dead Cover Letters: Great Letter Techniques and Samples for Every Step of Your Search.* (Avon, MA: Adams Media, 2008).

Wall Street Journal Careers site, "How to Write a Cover Letter," http://guides.wsj.com/careers/how-to-start-a-job-search/how-to-write-a-cover-letter/.

Dummies.com, "Cover Letters," www.dummies.com/how-to/business-careers/careers/Cover-Letters.html.

Purdue Online Writing Lab, "Cover Letters," http://owl.english.purdue.edu/engagement/index.php?category_id=34&sub_category_id=42.

LIBRARY RESOURCES

As with drafting or refining your résumé, you should look to your public library for help with writing cover letters. Check their website or ask a reference librarian what resources the library offers. Possibilities include classes or workshops, an ask-a-librarian appointment, or one-on-one consultations with career experts.

WRITING THE PERFECT LETTER, TOP TO BOTTOM

Once you get the hang of it, writing a cover letter is easy. You can follow this simple outline—just take it from the top and work your way down the steps.

Start at the Top

Always use a formal business letter style and format. (See example.)

Your Information:

As with any business letter, your name and contact information should appear at the top. If you're formatting a document, it's a good idea to use the same layout and font you use on your résumé. Otherwise, simply type it in below the date. Include the contact information the employer will need, especially phone number and e-mail address.

Date:

Unless your cover letter appears in the body of an e-mail message, date it. If you're writing your draft over the weekend, for example, use the date you plan to drop the letter in the mail so the letter looks as recent as possible.

Salutation:

Ideally, you will use the recipient's name, as in "Dear Mr. Brown:" Because few job postings include a person's name, try browsing the company website, LinkedIn, and other Internet sources to see if you can find the name of the current department head, hiring manager, or HR professional. If you can't find a name that you're certain will be the end reader, use something like "Dear Human Resources Professional:" or "Dear IT Manager:"

Anything but the frigid "Dear Sir or Madam:" or "To Whom It May Concern:"!

OPEN WITH YOUR STRONG SUIT

Start the body of your letter by identifying the position you're applying for. Don't assume the reader will know this; their organization may have multiple positions open. Other things to include in your first paragraph:

✦ If you've been referred by, or know someone, that the reader knows, mention their name right off the bat: "Your director of operations, Samantha Samuels, suggested I contact you. . . ."

✦ If you don't have an "in" or introduction, find a strong start. For example, showcase your knowledge of the hiring company or department, or of the industry. This is where the research that you'll learn to do in chapter 7 will really pay off!

THE MIDDLE MATTERS

Now that your first paragraph has caught the reader's attention, hit 'em with your sales pitch. The second paragraph should highlight your qualification, skill, or experience that makes you the best candidate for this particular job. Don't simply restate your résumé, but pull out one or two points and expand on them, with a focus on how they can be applied to the open position and that employer.

If you want to touch on multiple points, one way to stay concise is to use bullet points. This makes your letter shorter and easier to read.

MAKE YOUR CLOSING ARGUMENTS

Use your final paragraph for what direct marketers call a "call to action." Encourage the reader to contact you and let her know you're interested in the job. But if you have—or can get—the telephone number of the hiring manger or HR professional you are addressing, say that *you* will call *her* next week, and do it! If you can keep control of the contact rather than passively waiting by the phone, take advantage—just don't become a pest.

Include a "thank you" to the reader—for her consideration, for her interest, or for her prompt attention.

When signing off of a cover letter, use "sincerely" or "yours truly" above your signature. These are the most businesslike options.

Add a P.S. below your signature. Direct marketers know that a postscript stands out, and that letter-readers will skip down to read that first. So use that "last word" for something important.

ESSENTIAL WRITING TIPS

While you're drafting each cover letter, keep these tips in mind:

+ Keep it short. Each letter should be just one page with plenty of white space.
+ Whether you're e-mailing or mailing the letter, it's a good idea to refer to your attached or enclosed résumé—this directs the reader to look at that important document.
+ Try to avoid starting every line or every paragraph with the word "I." You don't have to twist your words too much to change "I can do this" and "I can do that" to "ABC Corporation's data entry department provides the perfect opportunity for me to . . ."
+ Keep using those keywords! Recruiter Jill Silman says her firm scans each cover letter with its résumé—and is included in a keyword search. "The cover letter and résumé are really treated as one document," she says.

FORMATTING YOUR COVER LETTER

Your cover letter should match your résumé. Use the same typeface and type size in both. If you have a graphical or fancy heading for your contact information at the top of your résumé, repeat it in your cover letter. Use the same margin widths.

And as with all business letters, your cover letter should be single-spaced.

EXAMPLE OF FORMATTED LETTER (Condensed for space)

October 12, 2011

Eva M. Thornton
1234 S. Bly Ave., Apt. 23
Baton Rouge, LA 49302
evamthornton@122.com
123/345/5678

Dear Human Resources Professional:

Your job posting on Batonrougejobs.com for a sales support associate sounds like a good fit for my skills and experience—especially given your company's recent acquisition of ABC Technology. As you can see by my enclosed résumé,

- ✦ I have experience supporting a sales team at TRG Industries, where we sold customized computer components for the restaurant industry. There I quickly learned the ins and outs of a new market, technical components and sales service.
- ✦ I am proficient in Microsoft Office software as well as Access, and have completed extensive coursework in Word and Access.
- ✦ My previous jobs working in retail sales gave me invaluable experience in customer relations, handling complaints, and working as a member of a team.

Please feel free to contact me by phone or e-mail. I'd be happy to come in to meet with you in person. Thank you for your consideration.

Sincerely,

Eva M. Thornton

P.S. Your posting requested that I state my salary requirements. At my last job I was earning $36,000 per year and shared my team's annual bonus. I am looking for a position that would offer a salary comparable to that.

Salary Requirements: Give Them What They Want

If the job posting calls for applicants to give their salary history or salary requirements, you'd better include it! Countless hirers and recruiters said that if they ask for this and don't see it, that résumé doesn't make the cut.

Your cover letter is the ideal place for this. (Consider using your valuable P.S. slot to convey the information.) To give yourself the most flexibility, give the most general information.

Your salary history might consist of:

"I started my last position with an annual salary of $43,000, and when I left I was earning $46,500."

Your salary requirements might state:

"I am looking for a position that offers a salary in the range of $43,000 to $50,000."

You will, of course, do your salary research before you state any requirements so that you're sure your expectations are realistic! (See chapter 9.)

E-MAILING YOUR COVER LETTER

When answering a job posting by e-mail, the body of your e-mail message serves as your cover letter. It's a good idea to draft the letter in a word-processing document so that you can easily edit, proofread, spell-check, and save it—and when you have a final version, then copy and paste that into your e-mail. Proofread one more time before sending to check line breaks and remove bullet points and other formatting that might not appear properly.

Other tips for using your e-mail as a cover letter:

+ E-mails often tend to be rushed, informal, and terse. Do not allow this with your "cover e-mail." You should still use formal language.
+ If your e-mail program allows, create an automatic e-mail signature that includes your contact information. This way you don't have to type it in every time.
+ If you don't use an e-mail signature, be sure to include your phone number *and* e-mail address in the body of the letter. Your call to action close is the perfect place for this.
+ Obviously, you won't sign your e-mail, but still use the business close "sincerely" or "yours truly," followed by your full name.

How to Handle Hard Copies

It's rare that you will end up mailing or giving a prospective employer a hard copy of your cover letter and résumé. But if you do, be sure to print both documents out on the same good quality paper, and remember to sign the cover letter!

If you're mailing your résumé and cover letter, fold both documents together and use a #10 envelope.

THE LAST WORD

When you come across a job opening that sounds like a great fit, it's natural to want to hurry up and get your application or résumé in fast. But slow down—take the time to do some research so that you write specific information or ideas related to that position into your letter. Make sure you understand current salary and benefits ranges for the position, too, so you can base any salary information on that research.

Then sit down and write a carefully crafted, pinpoint-specific, killer cover letter. Proofread it, proofread it again, and then, before you hit that send button or lick that envelope flap, remember to proofread it.

Mastering Twenty-First-Century Networking

> " "A very important tip that people forget about: you have to work your network. People hire based on relationships, so if you know anyone who works for a company with an opening, that can greatly increase your chances."
> **—Damone Virgilio, staff development manager at Memphis (Tennessee) Public Library** "

> " "Networking is *huge* now. The more people you meet, the more likely they will search for you. And of course you can do a lot of networking online."
> **—Dionna Keels, member of Society for Human Resource Management (SHRM) staffing management expertise panel** "

You may be able to find a great job all on your own. But it is much, much, *much* more likely that someone else—maybe a lot of someones—is going to personally connect you to that perfect job. So start working the power of networking, both face-to-face and online. Make connections with people you know and the people *they* know, and with people in the industry and the organizations you want to work in—and it's likely you'll connect to some major help in your job search.

What can networking do for you?

+ Lead to information on job openings not yet posted
+ Lead to an inside connection at a company who may put in a good word for you
+ Provide you with insights and ideas into an industry or profession that's new to you
+ Give you guidance in your job-search methods, including résumé review

" "When people come to us and I sit down with them, I tell them the top ways people find jobs these days are networking and through company websites."

—Barb Vlk, business librarian at Arlington Heights (Illinois) Public Library "

Best in Show—Networking

Benjamin, Susan. *Perfect Phrases for Professional Networking: Hundreds of Ready-to-Use Phrases for Meeting and Keeping Helpful Contacts Everywhere You Go.* (New York: McGraw-Hill, 2009).

Hansen, Katharine. *A Foot in the Door: Networking Your Way into the Hidden Job Market.* (Berkeley, CA: Ten Speed Press, 2008).

Levinson, Jay Conrad. *Guerrilla Networking: A Proven Battle Plan to Attract the Very People You Want to Meet.* (Bloomington, IN: AuthorHouse, 2009).

McKay, Harvey. *Dig Your Well Before You're Thirsty: The Only Networking Book You'll Ever Need.* (New York: Currency Books, 1999).

Pierson, Orville. *Highly Effective Networking: Meet the Right People and Get a Great Job.* (Pompton Plains, NJ: Career Press, 2009).

YOUR NETWORKING TOOLKIT

Tool #1: A Fine-Tuned Elevator Pitch

You've heard of an elevator pitch, right? It's a brief—no more than two-minute—explanation that you can state in the time it takes to share an elevator ride. Practice your own pitch, telling who you are and what you want, so you can be ready to introduce yourself clearly, succinctly and without rambling into why you lost your last job or how long you've been unemployed.

Tool #2: A Box of Business Cards

Have brand-new business cards printed for your job search. (It is a definite DON'T to use business cards from a previous or current position to look for a job!) It's cheap, easy, and fast to get hundreds of cards printed that you can use to network during your job search. These cards should include:

- Your name and the contact information you want potential employers to use. (Do not use your work phone or e-mail address, or your partyanimal@yahoo.com address!)
- The job title you want—or, if more practical, a general industry or profession. You want the card recipient to quickly understand what you're looking for when they come across your card days later.
- Three to six bullet points on the back that list your strengths
- If you have a website with additional information or an online portfolio, include your URL.
- Space for writing a personalized note.

Tool #3: A Well-Honed Strategy

The better you plan your networking, the better it will work for you. Take time to determine what types of people may best help you in your search, and where you might find them. For example, if you're looking for people who can help you get your foot in the door with an IT career, what groups or associations might they belong to? What meetings might healthcare administrators attend? When is the next national conference related to your industry coming to town? Do your research before you choose a local networking venue!

NETWORKING WITH THOSE YOU KNOW

Before you attend your first formal networking event, work your own network. Contact the following people in your life to let them know you're looking for a job, what type of job you want, and how they might help you.

- Extended family members
- Friends
- Neighbors
- Former work colleagues

+ Former classmates
+ Fellow members of your church, clubs, civic organizations, etc.
+ Everyone else you know

You might feel uncomfortable approaching people you haven't spoken to in a long time, or who may not seem appropriate to contact. But once you get over your initial apprehension, you'll find that businesspeople find networking a perfectly natural thing.

FOR INSTANCE . . .

"When I first decided to go freelance, I had only a few clients lined up. So I fearlessly listed all the people I knew who might hire me—then proceeded to call only the 'easy' ones. Within a year, I got phone calls from two of the people on my list who I had not had the nerve to call for work. Each one had heard through the grapevine that I was a freelancer, and had a project to offer! If I had only called those managers right away, I might have gotten even more work."

—Jane Jerrard, freelance writer, Chicago, Illinois

Use the Strength of Weak Ties

Ask your social network to spread the word of your job search to *their* networks. According to sociologist Mark Granovetter, author of "Strength of Weak Ties," the people who are most helpful to us are those we don't know well. Granovetter's theory posits that in marketing or politics, the weak ties enable reaching audiences that are not accessible via strong ties. Granovetter told *Forbes* magazine that "informal contacts" account for almost 75 percent of all successful job searches.

In other words, if your brother can't help you get a job, it's more likely that his buddy—or his buddy's buddy—might be able to.

NETWORKING GROUPS, EVENTS, AND MEETINGS

How do you find local networking opportunities? Ask a librarian, check a directory, or surf the web—or ideally, do all three. Your best bet is to find associations or networking groups affiliated with the career you're looking for. Join local chapters or groups, or just attend their meetings. There may be a fee for joining and/or one for attending, but if you choose the groups carefully, these are wise investments.

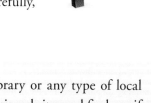

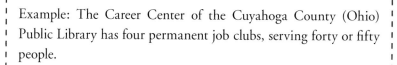

"You start with your local library or any type of local organization. Call them up or check their websites and find out if there are any networking groups or job clubs."
—Barb Vlk, business librarian at Arlington Heights Public Library (Illinois)

Example: The Career Center of the Cuyahoga County (Ohio) Public Library has four permanent job clubs, serving forty or fifty people.

If you join an association, make your membership pay off by getting involved. Volunteer to work on the newsletter, meeting programs, board of directors, or other areas. This will increase your visibility and expand your network within the group.

Online Resources for Finding F2F Networking

Browse the many groups included in the websites Meetup.com and LinkedIn to find local groups of like-minded professionals who meet in person:

✦ At www.meetup.com, you can enter your town and area of interest to find groups that meet regularly in-person. Whether your interest is "web development" or "skiing," the groups you find exist solely to help you meet and network with like-minded people in your area!

✦ www.linkedin.com also offers a multitude of groups, only some of which meet in person. Click on "groups" at the top of any LinkedIn page, then "Groups Directory." When you search the groups, select "Networking Groups" and type in the category and keywords that fit your job search.

66 "Associations geared toward your industry give you an opportunity to meet people, maybe volunteer, and make personal connections."

—Dionna Keels, member of Society for Human Resource Management (SHRM) staffing management expertise panel 99

Best in Show— Association-Locators

WebSites

Weddle's Association Directory, www.weddles .com/associations/index.cfm.

A free online listing of thousands of associations around the world by profession and industry with live links to each association's website.

Ip12'sResourcesbySubject,"Associations,"www. ipl.org/IPLBrowse/GetSubject?vid=13&cid=7

Books

Directory of National Trade and Professional Associations (Bethesda, MD: Columbia Books, 2007).

Encyclopedia of Associations (Thomson Gale, 2005).

JOB SUPPORT GROUPS

> "As far as resources, I've collected a list of networking groups in our area. And I start every [library] program and class by saying coming to this event is networking too."
> **—Barb Vlk, business librarian at Arlington Heights Public Library (Illinois)**

What librarian Vlk calls "the infamous networking support group" offers terrific networking opportunities as well as an ego boost. "That word *support* is key," says Vlk. "You need someone to talk to about your job search, and you need reinforcement that you're not alone and it's not your fault."

How does a job support group work? Here is an example of the groups run by Bob Podgorski, coordinator of the St. Hubert Job and Networking Ministry, which offers non-denominational job groups throughout the northwest suburbs of Chicago. Podgorski says,

Group networking typically involves being in a group of anywhere from six or seven people to thirty or forty people. Each individual provides an elevator speech—a two-minute overview of her skills, abilities, achievements and job desires—followed by a request for assistance from the group. Typically, contacts are sought, or help with identifying companies in key industries, or even suggestions of alternate industries where the person might apply their skills and background.

A résumé or handbill is passed around to the group so that everyone has your basic information and contact information. A handbill is preferred—this is a concise, to-the-point, one-page document that provides a section that lists target companies.

The real benefit of the group is the strength of weak ties theory: "People know people who know people," Podgorski points out. "A support group broadens your visibility to the point where you get the broadest distribution possible.

FOR INSTANCE . . .

Maybe a hairdresser in your job support group knows a woman who's married to a senior bank officer at the branch where you are looking for an opportunity. "Telling people in a group what you're looking for is your best chance of reaching a company—sometimes before positions are advertised," says Podgorski.

Job support groups work best when you target industries, occupations, and key company contacts that you'd like. You need to ask for help as precisely as possible in order to get the best help. Including a job title helps. It's a concise way for people to quickly understand what you want.

"Association meetings and industry networking events aren't necessarily (or likely to be) focused on job search," says Podgorski. "Job-search support groups are. Their entire goal is to get individuals to find jobs."

NETWORK THROUGH VOLUNTEERING

Another great way to target your networking is through volunteer work. While any community or civic volunteering will increase the number of people you meet, consider zeroing in on either gaining valuable professional experience, or demonstrating your skills:

+ Looking for a marketing position? Offer to write news releases, promote fundraising events, and create a marketing plan for the local charity you're interested in.
+ Aiming for a career transition to retail sales? Offer to man the counter at your local food pantry.
+ Not sure of your career path? Volunteer for a community or national charity, and meet professionals from all walks of life. Find out what they do for a living, what it's like and whether it would be a good fit for you.

You can add new skills or strengthen others through the right volunteer position:

+ Want to learn to sell? Offer to fund-raise!
+ Want to master public speaking? Volunteer to give one or more presentations to the local chapter!

✦ Want to gain some leadership experience? Sign up to lead a committee, or serve on the board!

Volunteering is also a great way to plug gaps in your work history. If you can point to some professional work you've done in the year you've been unemployed, it looks good!

STEPS FOR IN-PERSON NETWORKING EVENTS

Before You Go:

1. Craft—and practice—a one- or two-minute introduction of yourself and what you do or would like to do (your elevator pitch). This might be different for different networking opportunities.
2. Have a couple of conversation points ready—perhaps on the latest news within the industry. When in doubt, ask the other person about herself.
3. Set one specific goal before each event. Examples:

✦ Are you looking for a job lead?
✦ An information interview?
✦ Someone to review your résumé and job-search plan?
✦ Tips on breaking into the industry?

While You're There:

1. Keep plenty of your business cards on hand (literally—you can put your hand on one without fumbling in your purse or briefcase), along with a pen.
2. Work the room. No matter how shy or uncomfortable you may feel, approach people and introduce yourself.
3. Find the "movers and shakers." Use your powers of observation, the goodwill of the meeting's organizer or greeter, and ask

questions of others you approach to find the people at the event who are most likely to help you—whether you think they are the officers of the association, employees of certain companies you are prospecting, or "big names" in the industry.

4. Be efficient with your time and with others.' This includes coming prepared to politely disengage yourself from unproductive conversations.

5. Don't ask anyone to hire you. Instead, ask for their help and advice with your search.

6. Hand out your business card to everyone you meet, and ask for theirs. If you discuss anything you'd like to follow up on, jot down a note to yourself on their card.

When You Get Home:

1. Who did you meet? Look through the business cards you collected, and add any notes you might have missed while the event is still fresh in your mind.

2. Go to your LinkedIn profile and invite the most promising contacts you made to join your network. (See "online networking" below.)

3. Organize your contacts. Ideally, you should do this electronically so that your growing database of job-search contacts is searchable. You can use Microsoft Outlook or create an Excel spreadsheet. Include the person's contact information, title and company, where and when you met him (every time if ongoing), and any notes about his background or expertise that might aid your search.

4. Follow up if you said you would—or even if you didn't, in the case of the most valuable contacts you made.

5. Review the networking that you did, and what you'd like to do differently the next time you go out.

FOR INSTANCE . . .

Say you land an interview at the Promising Company. The name sounds familiar, so you search your electronic database of networking contacts to find the Promising manager you met a couple of months ago. You can leverage this connection a number of ways: contact her before your interview to reconnect, ask for her overview of the workplace; consider asking her to put in a good word for you—she may reap a finder's fee for doing so; and bring up her name during your interview to demonstrate your connection to the Promising Company.

Following up:

1. If you agreed to follow up with someone you met, call or e-mail the person within a day or two, while your encounter is still fresh in her mind.

2. Suggest a prescheduled phone call or an in-person meeting as an opportunity to discuss your goals. If she is amenable to a one-on-one meeting, suggest having coffee near her office or home, and pick up the tab.

3. Again, don't ask for a job—ask for advice, industry information, leads, etc. Sample questions:

✦ How do you/your company generally seek job candidates these days? Online job boards, or through recruiters?

✦ Can you recommend professional associations or industry networking organizations that I should join?

✦ What is your opinion of the state of our industry today?

4. Be sure to open that follow-up conversation with a big THANK-YOU, and end it with an offer or question about how you can help them. Don't be a user! Networking is a two-way street.

Here is what your networking contact tracking system might look like:

Name	Company	Title	Where met	Follow-up
Sandra Anders	ABC Corporation	Regional sales	5/12/10 library meeting	Send article on Google marketing
Sarah Jones	Meteor Marketing	Director of Sales	5/12/10 library meeting	None
Fred Fredericks	Premium Coffee Co.	Sales manager	May meeting— NSWA	Call for information int.

ONLINE NETWORKING

While face-to-face networking is crucial, you can turbo-boost the number of professionals you meet and connect with by using social media websites, online discussion groups, and other web-based tools.

Remember—the Internet provides many respected and relevant sites you can use to "see and be seen."

Sign Up Now!

Here are the basic sites to visit, check out, and sign up for in order to network online:

✦ LinkedIn: The undisputed champion of online networking for professionals

✦ Facebook: This highly personal site can be used to your advantage

✦ Meetup.com: This networking site can help you organize or join groups in your community.

✦ Online discussion forums on sites for appropriate professional associations, including "affinity groups" such as the American Assembly for Men in Nursing, or the California Association of Black Lawyers
✦ The website for your alumni association
✦ Twitter

Most, if not all, sites will require you to sign up with some personal information, and create a user name and password for future use. Remember to keep track of these names and passwords so that you can get back into a site once you've registered!

Best in Show— Online Networking

Crompton, Diane, and Ellen Sautter. *Find a Job Through Social Networking: Use LinkedIn, Twitter, Facebook, Blogs and More to Advance Your Career.* (Indianapolis, IN: JIST Works, 2010).

Jacoway, Kristen. *I'm in a Job Search—Now What???: Using LinkedIn, Facebook, and Twitter as Part of Your Job Search Strategy.* (Cupertino, CA: Happy About, 2010).

Vermeiren, Jan. *How to Really Use LinkedIn.* (Charleston, SC: Book-Surge Publishing, 2009).

websites/online articles:

"LinkedIn Tricks for Networkers, Job Hunters and Hirers" by Lisa Cullen for Time.com. http://workinprogress.blogs.time.com/2007/06/07/ linkedin_tricks_for_networkers/.

"Top 10 Social Media Do's and Don'ts: How (and How Not) to Use Social Media to Job Search" by Alison Doyle for About.com. http://

jobsearch.about.com/od/onlinecareernetworking/tp/socialmediajob-search.htm.

"Ten ways to use LinkedIn" by Guy Kawasaki (blog post). http://blog.guykawasaki.com/2007/01/ten_ways_to_use.html#axzz0nAh7w5bx.

"Blog Basics: How a Blog Can Boost Your Career" by Cara Scharf for Wetfeet.com. www.wetfeet.com/Experienced-Hire/Getting-hired/Articles/Blog-Basics—How-a-Blog-Can-Boost-Your-Career.aspx.

CONNECT TO THE POWER OF LINKEDIN

LinkedIn is a job-seeker's dream. It exists solely for business professionals to network with each other, and provides a wealth of information (sometimes available only for actual wealth) for those researching hiring managers and organizations.

With LinkedIn, you create a personal profile, then link to other people on the site to create your own network. You can only view complete profiles of (or send a message or "InMail" to) those you are personally connected to—but you can see basic identifying information for anyone on the site.

If you're not "linked" already, follow these steps:

1. Visit www.linkedin.com.
2. Take plenty of time to carefully craft your profile. This will serve as an online résumé, an introduction, and an identifier.
3. Use as many keywords as you can in your profile—it is searchable by other LinkedIn users, including recruiters and hiring managers!
4. Next, invite everyone you know to join your network: former and current work colleagues, bosses, friends, classmates, family, neighbors, etc. But focus on those who might be in a position to help you search: well-connected people, or anyone who has anything to do with your industry.

5. To find contacts you know, search through provided lists of company employees and university graduates. Also try browsing the connections of those you connect to, to see if you can find mutual acquaintances. Note that ethically, you can only connect to people you already know, even if you only met that person once.

6. When you invite someone to join your LinkedIn network, always include a personal note, no matter how brief.

7. Once your profile is complete and your personal network is up and growing, seek recommendations from some of your connections. Consider which of your acquaintances are most beneficial to your job hunt, then send each a brief but polite message through LinkedIn requesting a personal recommendation about specific skills, knowledge, and/or strengths. All recommendations will show up on your profile for visitors to see. An added benefit: if your former manager writes you a recommendation, all of *his* connections will be notified, drawing their attention to you!

8. Update your profile regularly, or post your latest accomplishment, activity, or thought. Those you are connected with will be notified of your new status, keeping you front-of-mind.

66 "LinkedIn is not the easiest thing to learn, but it includes a page that offers free tutorials on how to use it."

Barb Vlk, business librarian at Arlington Heights Public Library (Illinois)

Check with *your* local library to see if it offers workshops or tutorials on using LinkedIn or other social media for job-hunting. **99**

As you build your LinkedIn connections, you will be able to see second- and third-level connections. That is, the people that your connections are connected to, and the people that *those* connections are connected to. You can see at a glance the strength of weak ties when you see that your former work colleague is connected to a hiring manager at the company you want to work for.

JOB SEARCHES ON LINKEDIN

LinkedIn does include a job-search area (see chapter 3), but the true value of this site for a job-seeker lies in the wealth of organizational and employee information available, and the possibility of reaching out to connections of connections. In fact, each job posting includes an option to "find people in your network at [company]." You can ask your common connection for an introduction to that inside connection, or you can "upgrade" your LinkedIn account, meaning you'll pay a monthly fee for the ability to send a specific number of InMails to secondary connections. Such upgrades start at $24.95 a month for three InMail messages to "strangers" and a certain number of peeks at profiles.

FOR INSTANCE . . .

Congratulations! Your online job search landed you a coveted interview with Premium Corporation, a large company based in your city. Here are three ways to use the power of LinkedIn to prep for your interview:

1. Do you have any connections there? LinkedIn's search capability allows you to search by company. Type in "Premium Corporation" to find a list of all employees (past and present) on LinkedIn. The search results page will tell you right up front (literally) if you have any connections there, and if your connections have any connections there.

---

2. Get the basic dope. If you're searching for details on a larger company, that company page will reveal some basic information, including an overview statement, number of employees, revenue, and "recent activity," showing employee promotions, departures, and more.

3. Scope out the person or people you'll be meeting. If you have a name and/or job title of your interviewee, search them out. You won't be able to see complete profiles (unless you pay to upgrade your account), but you may be able to figure out chain of command, verify the job title and spelling of their names.

FACEBOOK: FOR FUN ONLY?

Facebook (www.facebook.com) is used primarily for personal, not professional, information-sharing and networking. However, you can—and should—incorporate it in your online networking plan to a certain extent. Here's how:

1. Posting on your Facebook "wall" is an efficient way to let everyone you've connected with know that you're looking for work. You can do this frankly, which gets the message across:

"Amy Anderson is . . . looking for an entry-level job as a receptionist. If you know of anything, please call or e-mail me!"

Or you can be more subtle—a good tactic if you plan to post gentle reminders throughout your job search:

"Amy Anderson is . . . prepping for a phone interview for a part-time receptionist gig. Keep your fingers crossed for me."

2. Use Facebook's search function to find specific organizations. Many businesses and associations now have their own pages, which can include a gold mine of information including insights into corporate culture, the very most recent happenings, and even specific job postings!

❝ "We just had a corporate recruiter do a program on Facebook. Now, they're not looking at people's Facebook pages, but they are posting jobs on their own page. LinkedIn has job listings too—and employers *will* go to LinkedIn to look at your information."
—Barb Vlk, business librarian at Arlington Heights Public Library (Illinois) **❞**

A WEALTH OF NETWORKING VIA MEETUP

Meetup.com describes itself as "the world's largest network of local groups." Members in more than two thousand different groups meet face-to-face every single day, all over the world. Some groups are based on hobbies, interests, even finding dates—and many are based on professional networking. Sign up for one or more appropriate Meetup groups and go to a meeting—it's a perfectly natural way to meet new people in your profession.

You can also use a specific group's Meetup.com page as a discussion forum, to connect with other group members, ask questions, etc.

Sample Meetup groups

Transitioning Professionals of Albuquerque
North Pittsburgh Professional Women's Network
Marketing Methods for Business Owners
Chicago Health Care Professionals Social Group

Online Discussion Forums

The number of online discussion forums devoted to specific topics is literally limitless—more are being formed every day, as people seek out new ways to connect and share information. To find specific forums best suited to help you network for a job, consider finding forums about job searches in general, the business world, and your target industry or profession.

Job-Search Forums

+ Monster.com
+ About.com Job Search Discussion Forum
+ Simply Hired (www.forums.simplyhired.com)

General Business Forums

+ Fast Company's Company of Friends (Fastcompany.com/cof)
+ Yahoo! Groups
+ Vault.com discussions

Industry-Specific Forums

Search on your industry (or profession) and "discussion forum" or "chat room"

It's Not Networking
If You Don't Comment!

Simply joining a Meetup group or your alumni association is *not* networking. Your real networking occurs when you add a comment or start a discussion in a forum, reach out to selected individuals and ask questions or offer advice, and generally showcase your professional know-how and experience.

Use these forums to post questions, share your own knowledge, or start an insightful discussion. This is a good way to introduce yourself as a member of the industry or profession, and can even serve as a real introduction to an in-person meeting.

TWEETING AND BLOGGING

If you want to cover all your bases with networking online, try using Twitter (twitter.com) and/or creating your own blog. The catch with both is that they can be time-consuming while the payoff is uncertain; the effectiveness of your communication depends on who is reading your posts.

Twitter is ideal for broadcasting short calls for help with your job search, giving updates, and more. It's free, you have to sign up (of course), and each tweet is limited to 140 characters, ensuring brevity. As with LinkedIn, you should look for business contacts to connect with (or "follow" in Twitter-speak). The more people you sign up to follow, the more followers you are likely to attract.

Twitter DOs and DON'Ts

DO start tweeting about business topics—load your tweets with keywords that might be searched on. You can post about the state of the industry, the latest business news, how you just mastered a new skill, etc.

DON'T post about your job search incessantly. No one wants to read that.

DO tweet when you need an immediate answer to a question: "Does anyone have a contact at Major Marketing?" "How do I dress for an interview with a graphic design firm?"

DON'T ask for a job.

DO offer your own tips, links, and entertainment—no one will follow you if all you do is ask for help!

In addition to tweeting your job search, you can search Twitter for posts on "job search," "résumé," "interviewing," etc. to find links to articles, advice, or just general news. There are even some random job postings on Twitter: to find them, search for "#job."

You can also create a **blog**, and write regular posts that demonstrate your expertise, skills, and insight in your chosen career field. It's unlikely that hiring managers or recruiters will find you through your blog, but it could serve as a valuable supplement to your résumé and cover letter in getting your foot in the door.

> "People don't know how to network—or they're shy. But you have to do it. No matter where you go, you could be talking one-on-one to the person who may give you that job lead. They may know of a job that's just opened up."
>
> **—Barb Vlk, business librarian at Arlington Heights Public Library (Illinois)**

THE LAST WORD

Keep in mind as you're searching the web for networking opportunities, posting comments on discussion forums and entering today's post for your LinkedIn profile, Facebook page, and Twitter, that you should limit the amount of time you spend in online networking. It's easy to devote hours of every day to your job search, but you'll do best if you set a time limit for yourself to avoid getting sucked into an afternoon of browsing. If necessary, set the alarm on your cell phone—or your kitchen timer—to allot a specific, reasonable amount of time to networking in one sitting.

Examining Potential Employers

All successful job-seekers must become expert researchers. How else will you figure out where to find the most relevant job openings, the employers most likely to hire you, and the details you need to arm yourself with before you walk in to your first interview?

This chapter focuses on one area of research: uncovering information about the specific organizations you want to work for. Whether you've already got an interview scheduled, or want to ID a company to cold call, the more you know about the organization in advance, the better off you'll be.

"I advise people to do a lot of research. Read anything and everything you can find about that company—and *then* *mention it* in your interview. Even if it's not local news, you can share general information or reviews you've read. Ideally, you can follow up the interview by sending the person a copy of what you mentioned. This makes you stand out from the other candidates."

—Bernice Kao, job/career specialist and job service outreach librarian at Fresno County (California) Public Library

LIBRARY RESOURCES

You may think you know how to research . . . but you've got a lot to learn. And who better to guide you than a librarian? Stop by your public library's reference desk and ask if a librarian-specialist can walk you through using available resources to investigate your potential employers.

IDENTIFYING POTENTIAL EMPLOYERS

Simply checking job listings every day is the most passive form of job hunting. One way to be more proactive in your search is to carefully consider which organizations you'd like to pursue as your next employer, and then contact those companies. Researching employers by location, industry, corporate stability, and other factors can help you focus your search—and possibly pursue an opportunity that has not been advertised yet.

There are three sets of tools you can use for this research:

1. Library Databases

Barb Vlk, business librarian at Arlington Heights (Illinois) Public Library, asks, "How do you know what companies to go to?" Check with your local library to see which databases it subscribes to that might contain company information. "You can call up your library and ask which databases are good for this type of research," urges Vlk. "There are a number of databases where you can find company information, often with live links so you can just click through to their website. Some libraries restrict their databases to their cardholders; others let anyone access them."

Barb's Best Databases

Vlk's top three databases for researching potential employers are:

1. **Reference USA**—"probably the best because it's the most comprehensive. It's really a phone book online. If I search for all the businesses here in Arlington Heights, I'm going to get around five thousand. That's because it will list every Panera Bread and McDonald's in town, along with home businesses. You can search by type of business and by number of employees. It's the best place to start."

2. **Million Dollar Directory** "is good too, although it only includes larger companies."

3. **Lexus Nexus Library Express Edition** "is a good place for getting news items on companies. Check this before you go to the interview, or to find something you can tie into your experience

in your cover letter. Just let the hiring manager know that you've done your research and you know who that company is."

Vlk adds, "All of these can be downloaded to Microsoft Excel, so if you're familiar with Excel, then you've got a really nice working list for a job searcher."

Factoid

Small businesses (those with 500 or fewer employees) have generated nearly two-thirds of all new jobs over the past fifteen years, according to the U.S. Small Business Administration in 2007.

2. Websites

Of course, the Internet provides plenty of information on companies by industry, location, etc. Try these sites to start:

Hoover's (www.hoovers.com) is the granddaddy of company information, now online with free, up-to-date, and detailed information on more than 50,000 companies. Includes privately owned companies, which is rare on other sites. You can access some information for free, but much of it is fee-based.

Jigsaw (www.jigsaw.com) is primarily a source for employee directories within companies, but you can browse their site by industry, company name, state, or city to find an extensive list of companies. While individuals' contact information may prove invaluable, you can also use Jigsaw as a starting point to develop a list of potential employers in your area, then check out each company's own website.

Top 100 Inc. 5,000 Companies by Industry (www.inc.com/inc5000/2007/lists/top100-industries.html) provides basic information on what they have found to be the "fastest growing" organizations within each industry.

Guidestar (www2.guidestar.org) includes a searchable directory of nonprofit organizations.

***Fortune's* list of best companies to work for**

(http://money.cnn.com/magazines/fortune/bestcompanies/2010/) is updated annually.

Price's List of Lists (www.specialissues.com/lol) is a database of ranked listings of companies, people, and resources.

3. Personal Contacts

Work your network. As you attend meetings and events, or introduce (and reintroduce) yourself to others during your job search, ask about what companies you should include in your search. If you're talking to someone in your targeted industry, ask where they work, where they've worked in the past, and which are the "local leader" companies in that industry.

And if you're talking to someone who is not in your targeted industry, it's still worth finding out if they have any contacts or knowledge about that field—you never know!

Best in Show—
Researching Companies

The Riley Guide: "How to Research Employers."
www.rileyguide.com/employer.html#tutor

Quint Careers' Guide to Researching Companies, Industries, and Countries. www.quintcareers.com/researching_companies.html

LIST YOUR CONTACTS, THEN CONTACT YOUR LIST

This research aspect of your job search should be an ongoing task; don't wait to compile a complete list of potential employers before you act. If you put in some time browsing a library database, or Hoover's.com, and come up with an organization you think is a good fit for your talents, act right away! Follow these steps:

1. Study the company's website before you do anything. (See "How to Use a Company's website" below.)

2. Check their website (and a few job listing sites too) to see if there are any open positions in your area. If there are, apply for the position(s).

3. Find the most likely hiring manager using Internet research, and consider how you might best contact that person. Options include e-mailing your résumé (or request for an information interview) or sending a snail-mail letter. Phone calls are rarely welcome interruptions, as are unscheduled in-person visits. But you might consider sending an e-mail that states you will follow up by phone, and then calling a few days later. This will turn your "cold call" into a warmer one.

LEARNING MORE ABOUT A COMPANY

The second aspect of researching an organization is when you've decided to contact a company about a job opening, or after you are invited to an interview. The timing on this type of research is crucial, because the more you know about the organization, the industry, the geographic region, and even the individuals you may interview with, the more likely you are to impress the hirers, stand out from your competition, and get the job!

When to research a potential employer:

✦ **Before** you write your cover letter and customize your résumé
✦ **Before** you visit a company at a job fair
✦ **Before** you contact a hiring manager for an information interview
✦ **Before** your initial job interview—including telephone interviews!

> "Do your research *before* you send out your résumé. That way your résumé will be custom-made to that job. Match your qualities listed in the résumé to the job ad—and come up with three stories for when you interview. I have my [job-seekers'] class write their résumé to a specific job opening for practice."
> **—Bernice Kao, job/career specialist and job service outreach librarian at Fresno County (California) Public Library**

WHAT YOU SHOULD LEARN—AND WHERE

OK—you've found a promising job opening, registered for a job fair, or earned an appointment for an interview, and you're ready to start your research on a specific organization. What information should you gather on the company you're targeting?

Start with the basics:

+ The history, size, and scope of the organization
+ Its financial health and stability
+ Any recent news involving the organization
+ The organizational chart for the department or location you'll be working in
+ The corporate culture

And don't forget to educate yourself on . . .

+ Current state of industry, area
+ Latest news in industry
+ Most recent changes in the organization (executives hired, layoffs, awards, etc.)

For a company's history, size, and scope, look . . . in the "about us" section of the **organization's own website**. If the organization you're targeting is owned by a larger corporation, has changed its name, or has a second identity, try a Google search on additional names to see what information you might unearth.

For financial health, look . . . at a number of financial sites. If the organization is publicly traded (that is, it is owned by stockholders), you can easily check its financial performance. Start with the **Edgar database** of the U.S. Securities & Exchange Commission (www.sec.gov). **Yahoo! Finance** (http://finance.yahoo.com) compiles financial news on specific publicly traded companies—just type the company name into the search field. Also check the **organization's own website** for an annual report, which will include the year's financial performance.

Nonprofit organizations as well as publicly traded ones may post their reports online.

For recent news, look . . . on sites for **industry trade journals, local newspapers**, and perhaps **professional associations**. A carefully worded general search may yield recent news articles and announcements as well.

For org charts and corporate culture information, look . . . on the **company website.**

HOW TO USE A COMPANY'S WEBSITE

Of course, you should take time to thoroughly review the website of the company you're targeting. Pay attention to these areas of information:

About Us/History/Mission: In addition to a broad overview of the company, you may be able to figure out values, corporate culture, and even key words to use in writing or conversation.

Products/Services: A great way to introduce yourself to what exactly the company does, and imagine how you might fit in. Memorize product names, or at least categories, before you interview.

What's New/Press Releases: Glean the latest news about the company for excellent points to bring up in an interview or cover letter. Past news provides an instant time line for developments, product releases, even new hires—and demonstrate what the company thinks is newsworthy.

Leadership/Staff Directory/Structure: Find out who the major players are as well as who you may be working with and/or for in the open position. Note the names and titles of all of the above before heading in for an interview.

HOW TO KEEP UP ON INDUSTRY NEWS

It's a good idea to read up on general news about your profession, industry, and area throughout your job search. That way you'll be knowledgeable and insightful on cue when you unexpectedly meet a potential contact, while you're networking and especially while you're applying for and interviewing for positions.

> "You just have to pay attention to your own industry. Read all media and talk to people at [networking events]—and expand your interests to the bigger picture."
>
> **—Bernice Kao, job/career specialist and job service outreach librarian at Fresno County (California) Public Library**

Here is the bare minimum of industry research and news reading you should do throughout your job search:

1. Select one to three sources of industry-specific news (most likely trade journals) and at least skim every issue or update. If a publication is not available online for free, see if you can sign up for a trial subscription, borrow hard copies from a subscriber you know, or consider sharing the cost of a subscription with one or more fellow job-seekers.

2. Bookmark the website of a trade association. Check for recent updates to discussion forums or press releases. If you're a member, you may be able to get automatic news e-mails.

3. Join a profession- or industry-specific group on LinkedIn, and monitor the discussion forums.

4. Scan the headlines in your local or national newspaper every day. (Do this online for free.) This will prepare you for "small talk" at networking events or targeted comments in an interview situation. Job hunters can sometimes be isolated—demonstrate that you know what's happening in the world!

HOW TO USE LINKEDIN

More and more companies are adding a corporate profile on LinkedIn, with basic (but valuable!) information. Perhaps most important, you can see which employees are on LinkedIn and whether you have any first-, second- or third-level connections.

Find companies through people's profiles, or search LinkedIn for a company profile by name or keyword.

You can also choose to "follow companies" on LinkedIn, which enables you to receive automatic updates on changes to the profile, new developments, and job openings.

HOW TO LEARN FROM EMPLOYEES

Several websites offer information and insights into companies from current or past employees. All organizations are not included, of course, and remember to take comments with a grain of salt—a disgruntled employee may be settling a score. Try these:

Glassdoor.com lets employees post reviews of the companies they work for.

Vault.com's "Employer Reviews" (www.vault.com/wps/portal /usa/companies) give you a peek at insiders' comments on current and former employers. You need to create an account and log in to view many of these.

"Use your research to connect. When you read a news article where someone is quoted, write to that person to let them know you agree or disagree with what they said. Be a little aggressive, be alert, and connect to your own interest."

"Build your own network so people will know you."

—Bernice Kao, job/career specialist and job service outreach librarian at Fresno County (California) Public Library

Off-Line Research

Bernice Kao recommends doing some in-person research using what she calls "guerilla networking" techniques:

"See if you can find an inside source within the company. Maybe you're in a coffee shop or a [restaurant] near the company and you see someone wearing the corporate nametag. Ask them for a couple of minutes of their time—and buy their coffee. Tell them you're interested in the company and ask questions. Get their name, and give them your business card. It may just work out that when there's a job opening, they can deliver your résumé to the personnel office."

If this is too aggressive for you, at least ask the professionals in your network if anyone has information on the specific organization you're targeting. You may find out important information on corporate culture, history of layoffs, etc.

RESEARCHING INDIVIDUALS

Once you've got a specific organization in your sights, remember to include the hiring managers and other potential interviewers in your research. Why?

+ So that, when you are contacting a company for an unadvertised or "blind" job opening, you can address (and customize) your cover letter and résumé to a specific hiring manager. Use this tactic carefully, as some people may not appreciate your circumventing the HR department.
+ To make networking easier. If you want an information interview from a specific company, you can find out the most appropriate person to talk to.
+ For interview prep. When you haven't been told whom you'll be meeting with, you can make a best guess.

The two main places to look up titles, names, and contact information for employees within a company are that company's website and LinkedIn. You might also try a Google search on the person's name (if you know it) and company to see if any news items come up.

Use Your Information Wisely

If you find out details about your interviewers beyond their title and name, be tactful in how you use it. It's not a good idea to blurt out, "I Googled you!" as this might be seen as intrusive. But if you know the

HR professional you're talking to went to your alma mater, find a way to bring up the name of your school.

And keep in mind, if you're going in for an in-person interview (or even a telephone interview), it is likely that the interviewer has also checked *you* out on LinkedIn and through a general Google search.

THE LAST WORD

As you gather your research on organizations you apply to or are considering applying to, keep those notes handy. Consider creating a folder (paper or electronic) for each company you research, and keep it even if you stop pursuing that particular organization (or vice versa). Here's why: The company you're targeting today may be one of the main competitors of a business you interview with tomorrow, and it might come in handy to walk in armed with some information about that!

Honing Your Interview Skills

Those who have been job hunting for a while know that just getting a call for a first interview feels like you've met your goal. But that phone call is just the beginning of a new phase of the search. Interviewing for a job entails a lot of work: research, careful consideration, practice, and preparation. Because when you've put in the hours and effort to reach that first goal of an interview, you don't want to blow your chances!

> " "The only purpose of your résumé and of interviewing is to *be memorable*. So go in and tell your story, and connect yourself to the job and their company."
> **—Bernice Kao, job/career specialist and job service outreach librarian at Fresno County (California) Public Library** "

Best in Show—Interviewing

Beshara, Tony. *Acing the Interview: How to Ask ana Answer the Questions That Will Get You the Job.* (New York: AMACOM, 2008).

Oliver, Vicky. *301 Smart Answers to Tough Interview Questions.* (Naperville, IL: Sourcebooks, 2005).

Burns, Dan. *The First 60 Seconds: Win the Job Interview before It Begins.* (Naperville, IL: Sourcebooks, 2009).

Schuman, Nancy. *The Job Interview Phrase Book: The Things to Say to Get You the Job You Want.* (Avon, MA: Adams Media, 2009).

LIBRARY RESOURCES

Does your public library offer classes or workshops in interviewing skills? What about one-on-one practice sessions or consultations? You may think such services aren't part of a library's mission, but many public libraries are partnering with local job service organizations, finding skilled volunteers, or training librarians to help with steps like interviewing so that they can help out the job-hunters in their communities.

So call your library, visit its website, or stop in to see what help it might offer with interview prep, planning, and practice.

TYPES OF INTERVIEWS

It's true: there may be more than one type of interview involved in your job search. Whether you've requested an information interview, been asked to a participate in what is clearly a prescreening telephone call with a recruiter, or are going for the whole enchilada—the one-on-one, suit-and-tie, formal first interview—prepare thoroughly for each interview and always act in a businesslike manner. For more particulars on each type, read on.

INFORMATION INTERVIEWS

An information interview is different from a standard job interview. You should try to set up your own information interviews when you're trying to break into a field (as a new graduate or as a career-changer). You want to pinpoint someone who is established in that field—with the purpose of learning his insights into the state of the industry in your area, typical duties and responsibilities, skill set and education needed, and just about anything else that might help you target your search.

Not only can you learn a lot from an information interview, it is a powerful way to build your network. You might even get a job offer! An added benefit: information interviews allow you to practice for interviews and get comfortable with the format, without the pressure of trying for a specific job.

Who?

Whom should you ask for an information interview? If possible, try to set up several. Start with people you know from your personal network, then consider professionals you've met while networking for a job. Then browse listings of professional associations: board members and committee chairs are good bets for industry insiders who are willing to give up their time to help others. Consider only people who have worked in your target industry for at least several years; managers or executives are best.

How Long?

Because this interview is a favor to you, keep it short—half an hour at the very most. Use every minute of that time to get the information you want: that means taking time well in advance to plan what you want to cover. Consider what would benefit you most, and focus on one or two areas such as those listed under "What to Discuss?" below. For best results, let your interviewee know in advance what area you'd like to learn about.

What First?

Treat an information interview as you would a "real" job interview. That means:

+ Doing your research on the company in advance
+ Having questions and statements ready and rehearsed for a smooth conversation
+ Preparing and bringing at least two copies of your résumé (and your portfolio)
+ Dressing appropriately
+ Starting the meeting by exchanging business cards: now the professional has your contact info at hand (and you have hers)

What to Discuss?

What do you want to know the most about? Possibilities include:

+ What is it like to be a typical fill-in-the-blank worker? What are the job responsibilities and duties, and skills and knowledge required?

- ✦ How's my job-search strategy? Have the professional review what you're doing, where you're looking, and your résumé and experience.
- ✦ What is the state of the industry? Cover job outlook, salaries, changes coming up, major players in the area.

Information Interview DOs and DON'Ts

DON'T ask for a job in an information interview. People are willing to give you their time because they expect you to *not* do this. (But if someone offers you a job interview, an internship, or a position at the company, that's fine!)

DO ask for suggestions (or recommendations) of who to contact for a job, or ask her to do some light networking on your behalf.

DON'T let the established professional take control of the conversation. To ensure you cover what you want to discuss, begin the meeting with a brief introduction and explanation of what you'd like to learn during the meeting.

DO ask your interviewee if you can contact her again within a couple of weeks to see if she has any ideas for your job search.

DON'T ask for a job. (We can't stress this enough!)

DO take notes. Jot down names of individuals and companies that might be job leads, write down their advice, and mark up a copy of your résumé if the person reviews it.

TELEPHONE INTERVIEWS

A hiring company or recruiter may conduct the first interview over the telephone, as this is more time-efficient for the interviewer (and you, too!). Here is what a professional recruiter has to say about phone interviews:

"The trend right now is to do a phone screen first," says Dionna Keels, a member of the SHRM (Society for Human Resource Management) staffing management expertise panel. "The goal is for the recruiter to be sure they're comfortable bringing a person in to meet with the hiring manager, without wasting anyone's time. Phone screens are almost a weeding-out process.

"A phone interview really is a first interview—so don't make the mistake of thinking it's not important," Keels stresses. "Do your preparation before the call. Do some research on the company you're interviewing with."

She encourages job interviewees to make it easier on the other person by holding a two-way conversation—which demonstrates your intelligence and personality. "Ask questions and find out more about the [job opening]," she recommends. "Your personal skills are very important over the phone. Talk openly about your experience and skills; have a real conversation."

Keels explains that what the telephone interviewer is after is proof that your work experience is a good match for the opening. "But they may also be doing a culture screen. They want to find out what you're looking for and see if it's a match," she says. How do you "ace" a culture screen? Make it part of your pre-interview research. Keels says, "If you go to the company's career page on their website, they may have videos and information that describe their culture. You may also find an HR professional through LinkedIn or the website, and call them up to explain that you're interviewing for a position there and have a couple of questions about the corporate culture. Also, ask anyone you know who has ever worked there. Look for employee blogs . . ."

In a way, telephone interviews are easier than in-person interviews because you can refer to notes or an outline when answering (or asking) questions. Have a copy of the résumé you sent in, and highlight the areas you'd like to talk about.

TIP: BERNICE KAO HAS TWO RECOMMENDATIONS FOR SPEAKING WELL ON THE PHONE: SMILE WHEN YOU SPEAK, AND PLACE A MIRROR WHERE YOU CAN SEE IT. CHECK YOUR EXPRESSION IN THE MIRROR WHEN YOU ANSWER THE PHONE AND THROUGHOUT THE INTERVIEW TO ENSURE YOU ARE SPEAKING CLEARLY AND NATURALLY—AND PUTTING THAT SMILE IN YOUR VOICE.

"Phone-Plus-Video" Interviews

According to an article in *Time* magazine, job interviews via computerized video-chats are growing in popularity—especially for interviewing out-of-state job candidates. In "How Skype Is Changing the Job Interview," Barbara Kiviat offers pointers for preparing yourself and your "set" to appear on-screen at www.time.com/time/business /article/0,8599,1930838,00.html#ixzz0ffanZJBc.

TIP: WHETHER YOU'RE SCHEDULING A TELEPHONE INTERVIEW, A FIRST INTERVIEW, OR A FOLLOW-UP INTERVIEW, MAKE SURE YOU GET THE DETAILS. IF YOUR CONTACT DOESN'T OFFER YOU THE INFORMATION, ASK HOW MANY PEOPLE YOU'LL BE MEETING WITH AND WRITE DOWN EVERYONE'S NAME AND TITLE. ASK FOR AN ESTIMATED TIME FRAME (WILL YOU BE THERE ONE HOUR OR ALL AFTERNOON?), IF YOU WILL BE EXPECTED TO TAKE ANY TESTS (ASSESSMENT, SKILLS, OR SOFTWARE TESTS). FINALLY, MAKE SURE YOU UNDERSTAND WHERE TO SHOW UP, INCLUDING THE FLOOR NUMBER AND WHOM TO ASK FOR WHEN YOU ARRIVE.

IN-PERSON INTERVIEWS

The key to a successful in-person interview is preparation. That includes doing
your research on the company and industry
(chapter 7), and thoroughly practicing interviews. Part of your practice should include

+ Researching, brainstorming, and asking professional friends to
  come up with likely topics that will be covered, such as your
  strengths and weaknesses, your ideal day at the job, etc.—and
  then decide how you want to answer those. "But don't try to
  guess interview questions and then memorize answers," warns
  Kao. "It's not going to sound like you."

+ Come up with real anecdotes, examples, results, and challenges
  from your previous work that you would like to mention. Then
  write them down and/or say them out loud a few times. Memorize any percentages, years, etc. you'd like to include. "Practice
  telling your stories beforehand," urges Kao. "Make sure each
  one illustrates a skill. You can practice short speeches very casu-
  ally, by telling a friend."

+ In order to conquer nervousness, ask a friend to hold a practice interview with you. "Practice each interview as if your life
  depends on it. Then treat the real interview as if it's another
  practice," advises Kao. "It's fine to be nervous when you're interviewing—but practicing will help with this. You have to practice over and over in order to gain confidence."

+ You can also try rehearsing your stories, anecdotes, etc. in front of
  a mirror, or even videotape yourself. Check your body language:
  do you look engaged, interested, and vital? Try leaning forward,
  keeping an open expression on your face, and uncrossing your
  arms.

What to Wear

These days, company dress codes range from business suits to blue jeans, making it difficult to know what to wear to a job interview. Jill Silman, SPHR, vice president at Meador Staffing Services and a spokesperson for the Society of Human Resources Management (SHRM), offers a good guide:

"Dress for the job. The whole interview is to prove you fit in; you want your clothes to help send this subconscious message to your interviewer. If you have to, stalk the company and see how people are dressed as they come out for lunch. If they all look like an ad for the Gap, you don't want to wear a suit, hose, and heels to your interview."

Silman says its OK to call the company's human resources before the interview to ask about the dress code for employees. "And if you're in doubt, you should dress up, not down."

Kao adds some good advice: No matter what you plan to wear, "Get used to your interview outfit," she says. "Practice wearing the whole outfit while standing, walking, and sitting. Never wear the outfit for the first time to an interview unless you want to look like a robot."

FOLLOW-UP INTERVIEWS

If your first interview goes well, you may be asked back for a second—and possibly a third—meeting. These follow-up interviews are likely to include more or different interviewers, as you are scoped out by all the key players.

Every company has its own procedure, but you may be offered the job as early as the end of the second interview—so be prepared beforehand to negotiate your salary and other terms. (Chapter 9 will help you plan for this.) Or you may be invited back for a third or even fourth time.

Treat all follow-up interviews much like your first interview; don't slack on review of your previous research and repeat your preparation. You should have noted the anecdotes and accomplishments you mentioned during all subsequent interviews, so review that information as well. You don't want to repeat a long anecdote to the same person a second time! Instead, consider what you didn't get a chance to say, or a point you didn't get a chance to sell, and try to work that into your conversation.

Keep in mind that if you passed the first interview, subsequent meetings may be to see if you are a good fit for the personality or culture of the company, so the questioning may be more personal: What would you do in this situation? How do you handle conflict? What types of activities do you enjoy in your off-hours?

> **TIP:** BE SURE TO ASK MORE QUESTIONS IN FOLLOW-UP INTERVIEWS; YOU WANT TO HAVE ALL THE INFORMATION YOU NEED TO MAKE A DECISION AND START NEGOTIATING!

PANEL INTERVIEWS

Don't be too surprised if your first or second interview for a job is conducted by a panel of managers or employees. "Many companies are using panel interviews to save managers' time," says Keels. "Also, a lot of companies feel that in a  panel interview, the interviewers can feed off each others' questions, and this makes them better interviewers and keeps them more comfortable."

Make sure you ask who all you'll be interviewing with when you set up the appointment, so that you can be prepared to face a panel or group if necessary. Kao recommends that at a panel interview, you should address and thank the person who asks the first question, then go around the panel while you talk until you come back to the first panelist. Continue to "rotate" your attention as you answer for each question.

Juggling Interviews and a Job

If you're employed and looking for a new job, it can get tough to be discreet about taking time off for interviews. If you don't want your current employer to know that you're looking, these are your options:

+ Take a day or half-day off work. This will allow you to dress and prepare appropriately. The downside: if you have multiple interviews, that's a lot of time off!

+ Try to schedule in-person interviews for first thing in the morning, or at the end of the day, to avoid taking too much time off. You can ask for an hour or so off for "an appointment" or "personal business."

+ Consider asking the interviewing company if you can come in (or phone in) after business hours. They should understand that you may not be able to take time off from your job—particularly if you've already been in for one or two interviews.

If you don't want your supervisor to know you're interviewing, be sure to mention this to everyone you interview with, to make sure no one lets the cat out of the bag until after you've accepted a job offer!

WHAT TO ASK, ANSWER, AND SAY

A lot of people have trouble talking about themselves and their accomplishments. Some have trouble simply talking when under pressure. That's why it's important to practice interviewing: what you'd like to say,  how you'll respond to questions on the fly, and what you want to ask.

Kao coaches job hunters at her library every day, and based on her extensive experience, she says, "Don't mumble. Take your time while talking, and pause . . . Pauses are a way to turn an interview into a relaxed conversation. They encourage dialogue instead of a lecture." Another tip: "Talk for two minutes at a time—no more. Let them ask for more information if they want it."

> **TIP:** PART OF YOUR PREPARATION FOR AN INTERVIEW SHOULD BE SELF-INTROSPECTION. THAT MEANS CONSIDERING AND KNOWING YOUR GREATEST STRENGTHS AND HOW THEY MATCH UP TO THE OPEN POSITION, YOUR PERSONALITY, YOUR STYLE OF WORK, AND YOUR WORK VALUES.

TAKE CONTROL OF THE INTERVIEW

Try to get the interviewer to talk first—even if it's just a brief overview of the open position. The more she tells you about the position, department, and organization, the better you can tailor your own comments to demonstrate what a great fit you are.

If the interviewer jumps right in by asking you to talk about yourself, lob the ball back into his court with a request like, "If you don't mind, can you first tell me a little about the position, so that I can better describe how my experience might fit here?" Then you can launch into your concise description of your experience, skills, and qualifications. This question offers a golden opportunity to highlight what you had planned to say to sell yourself—so do some planning and practicing, and be ready for it!

TELL A STORY

Kao is a proponent of job hunters being proactive while interviewing. This entails planning and practicing specific "stories" to tell while you're being interviewed. Formulate these stories based on the research you've done on the organization and the open position, to highlight areas that fit well with what you've learned. Your stories might include:

✦ A specific accomplishment from your most recent job: how you cut your department's budget by 23 percent last year; how you upgraded the customer-service software system; or how you wooed a new corporation into becoming the company's largest customer.

✦ An enthusiastic description of recent learning: the workshop you attended on a new industry-specific software package; the book you just finished on teamwork.

✦ An event that demonstrates a personal skill: how you handled an unexpected challenge; how you successfully managed a team of colleagues; how you juggled two jobs while your manager was on maternity leave.

✦ An anecdote that showcases your work values: how you mentored a new employee; how you volunteer in your professional association.

"Think of ways to communicate your value, how you can help your future employer," says Kao.

SHOW OFF YOUR RESEARCH

You did the hard work of researching the hiring organization and industry—don't forget to let your interviewers know!

Find a way to work your knowledge of the company and of the latest industry news into the conversation. Better yet, share your personal insights and opinions on that news. "They want to find out what you know that *they* don't even know yet," says Kao. "So talk about news items, industry trends, new technology as it relates to their business. You want to be the person who can tell them something that none of the other candidates can."

> "Never say 'I don't know.' Instead, say something like, 'I'm not too familiar with this subject, but let me tell you about . . . ' and go on to relate a story about how you mastered a new skill, or how your experience fits with the overall subject."
> —Bernice Kao, job/career specialist and job service outreach librarian at Fresno County (California) Public Library

Read Real-Life Interview Questions

Visit Glassdoor.com to read information posted about companies by actual interviewees, including real-life interview questions. You can find specific companies by profession/industry. Individuals post how they were initially approached by a company, what their interview process was like, and one or two examples of interview questions they were asked.

ASK QUESTIONS

Any job interview should be a two-way conversation. That means not only should you reply to questions, but ask some of your own. This demonstrates that you're curious about the open position and the company, that you understand the industry, work, structure, etc., and that you have a unique mind!

✦ Ask questions to clarify details you find unclear.

✦ Ask questions that demonstrate your own values and work culture: Does teamwork play a big part in the work style here? Do you value independence in your staff?

✦ Interview the interviewer: Why does he like working there, or why has he been there so long? What does he see as the department's strengths or weaknesses?

✦ Don't pretend to understand something you don't! Ask for definitions or explanations.

Two Interview Musts

Unless you decide that you really don't want the job you're interviewing for, there are two things you should use to close every interview:

1. Let them know you want the job. State clearly and directly that you want the position.

2. Find out what the interview process is. It is perfectly acceptable to ask questions to clarify the next step and when you should expect to hear from them. You can also ask how many candidates they're interviewing.

66 "It's all right to ask, 'How did I do?' You can even ask 'What else do you want to know about me in order to choose me for this position?'"

—**Bernice Kao, job/career specialist and job service outreach librarian at Fresno County (California) Public Library**

99

TESTING, TESTING, 1–2

Many organizations use some type of test to help qualify job candidates. At some point in the interviewing process, you may be asked to take:

+ An assessment test: Typically multiple-choice in format, these tests are designed to reveal your personal characteristics, values, etc., which lets the hirer know whether you are ethical and honest or whether you are a good match for their corporate culture.
+ A skills test: depending on the job you're applying for, you may be tested on knowledge of a specific software program, your writing skills, or math abilities.
+ A typing test: how many words per minute can you type?
+ A drug test: if the company requires drug screening, you may need to pass a drug test as a last step in the employment process.

Do your best to find out about any tests beforehand, so that you know what you'll be expected to do during the interview.

AFTER EACH INTERVIEW

Whew—the interview's over! That hurdle has been crossed, but you're not finished yet—you have a few follow-up tasks:

1. Take notes. As soon as possible, write down your impressions of the company, the job, and the interviewers for your own future reference. And make sure you have the names and titles of everyone you spoke to.
2. If the organization asked for references, contact those people immediately to notify them that they may soon be hearing from your prospective employer. If appropriate, remind them or coach them on what to emphasize about you.

3. Send a thank-you to anyone who might have referred you for the interview, letting him know how it went.

4. More important, send thank-you notes to your interviewers.

Give Thanks

Sending a prompt, succinct, and well-written thank-you note or letter to each person you interviewed with is a crucial step in your job-search process. Why? Because it is one more opportunity for you to make an impression and stand out from your competition, to sell your best qualifications, to prove you are an excellent match, and to ask for the job.

Here are the rules of writing thank-yous:

✦ Write a separate (and unique) note to every person you interviewed with.

✦ Send your notes within twenty-four hours of the interview.

✦ It's acceptable to e-mail a thank-you note, but writing or typing one and mailing it is better. A handwritten note is best used for a very brief communication, such as when you are thanking each of the four staff members you met with in addition to the department manager. (The manager may warrant a longer, typed letter.)

✦ Send a thank-you even if the interview did not go well or if you know you are no longer in the running for the position. Thank the interviewers for their time and consideration.

✦ Keep it brief—state your thanks, give one highlight of your accomplishments or one reference to a point that came up during the interview, and state your interest in the job.

> **TIP:** KAO RECOMMENDS, "FOLLOW UP ANY WAY YOU CAN THINK OF. TRY TO BE A MEMORABLE CANDIDATE. MENTION SOMETHING UNIQUE IN EACH THANK-YOU NOTE THAT YOU HAVE DISCUSSED DURING THE INTERVIEW. IT IS **OK** TO ENCLOSE ARTICLES YOU TALKED ABOUT, OR SOME EXTRA WRITINGS YOU HAVE DONE. BUT NOT PHOTOCOPIES OF YOUR AWARD OR TROPHIES!"

> **TIP:** IF YOU'RE GOOD AT WRITING ON DEMAND, HERE'S SOME GREAT ADVICE FROM SUSAN STRAYER OF SUSANSTRAYER.COM: "BRING BLANK THANK-YOU NOTES [WITH YOU TO THE INTERVIEW]. WRITE THEM IMMEDIATELY AFTERWARDS AND ASK RECEPTIONIST TO HAND-DELIVER—A HUGE **WOW.**"

Checking In

It's OK to check in on the status of your candidacy if you don't hear back from the interviewer. If you asked—and were told—that the hiring decision should be made within two weeks, contact the company a couple of days before that estimated deadline. If you don't know the time frame, wait about a week before making contact.

Call or e-mail the person you interviewed with to say thank you again and restate your interest in the job. You can leave this information in a voice mail message—but only call once to leave your message. If you keep hanging up on the person's answering message, they may see your number come up on Caller ID multiple times, which makes you look like a stalker.

If you still don't hear back after your first follow-up e-mail or voice mail, try again a week later. If you don't get a reply to your second message, you're not likely to hear back about the job. It's time to stop trying to contact them and move on with your job search.

THE LAST WORD

Interviewing for a job can be a nerve-wracking experience—especially for a job-hunter who is eager to be employed and put all the hard work of the search behind him. But try to relax and enjoy the interview portion of your search. It will help make you a better interviewee, and it will allow you to take a close and objective look at your potential employer while you're on the premises, and get a good feel for what it would be like to work there.

Negotiating the Best Pay and Benefits for Your New Job

Wise job-hunters will be ready and willing to negotiate salary and benefits when the appropriate time comes. Those who aren't prepared with solid research, industry knowledge, and confidence in their position are likely to lose out. And as negotiation expert Cheryl Palmer points out, once the opportunity for negotiating the terms of your new job is over, you'll never be able to make up the difference between what you get and what you could have had.

> "It's critical to practice negotiating. You may read books on the topic and understand the concept of negotiating, but it's a different story when your living is on the line."
> **—Cheryl Palmer, CECC, negotiation expert and president of Call to Career**

Best in Show—Negotiating

Fisher, Roger, and William L. Ury. *Getting to Yes: Negotiating Agreement Without Giving In.* (New York: Penguin, 1991).

Miller, Lee E. *Get More Money on Your Next Job . . . in Any Economy.* (New York: McGraw-Hill, 2009).

Wegerbauer, Maryanne. *Next-Day Salary Negotiation: Prepare Tonight to Get Your Best Pay Tomorrow* by (Indianapolis, IN: JIST Works, 2007).

Pinkley, Robin L., and Gregory B. Northcraft. *Get Paid What You're Worth: The Expert Negotiators' Guide to Salary and Compensation.* (New York: St. Martin's Griffin, 2003).

Garlieb, Stacie. *My Job Offer Negotiation Skills Are Solid (I Think) . . . So Why Didn't I Get Anything I Asked For?* (Charleston, SC: CreateSpace, 2010).

QuintCareers, "Salary Negotiation and Job Offer Tools and Resources for Job-Seekers," www.quintcareers.com/salary_negotiation.html.

Salary.com, "Negotiation Clinic," www.salary.com/Articles/ArticleDetail.asp?part=par186.

Susan Ireland's Resume Site, "Salary Negotiation Skills," http://susanireland.com/interview/salary-pay.

WHY NEGOTIATE?

If you're uncomfortable talking about money or asking for what you want, don't worry—go ahead and do it. Employers and HR professionals *expect* you to negotiate your starting salary. It's very rare that the first package offered—pay and benefits, that is—is fixed. So think of it as a starting point, and reach higher. Basic tips for successful negotiation include:

+ Have a solid grasp of what is realistic in terms of pay, benefits, and perks for the type of job you've been offered.
+ Also understand where you fit in the range of experience, skills, and value.
+ Let the other person begin. This ensures it's the right time to negotiate—and you hold the advantage if the employer names their figure first.
+ If negotiations reach a point where the final salary offer is still low, move on to negotiate for more or better benefits.

If you don't negotiate for what you want at this stage of accepting employment, Palmer warns, "You're likely to leave several thousand dollars on the table. And you'll never make that money up."

TIMING FOR MONEY TALK

The appropriate time to talk money (and benefits) is one of the firm rules in job interviewing. While the topic of pay may come up early—in a request for your salary history or requirements along with your résumé, for instance—the rock-solid rule is, don't bring up the subject until the employer makes you a job offer.

It's important to understand that that initial question is not part of salary negotiation or discussion, but simply to see if you fall in the general range of what they're paying.

> **TIP:** IF ASKED TO SUPPLY YOUR CURRENT OR PREVIOUS SALARY, DON'T LIE! IF YOU'RE HIRED AND THE LIE IS FOUND OUT, THIS IS LEGAL GROUNDS FOR TERMINATION.

DOs and DON'Ts for Talking Money

DO be prepared to start negotiations as soon as your second interview—though the topic may not come up until the third or fourth interview. (See chapter 8.)

DON'T ask about salary during your interviews. "It's not considered appropriate," says Palmer. "It's expected that when you get the job offer, you'll have done your research and be prepared to negotiate."

DO have any notes on your salary research ready to reference during discussions.

DON'T accept a job, salary, or benefits that you don't want.

DO ask for time to consider the final offer once you've reached an agreement on salary and benefits. It's acceptable to request a day or two to consider the final offer.

HOW JOB NEGOTIATION WORKS

Every organization has its own time line and process for hiring new employees, depending on its size and agility, procedures and protocols, and the difficulty of finding the best candidate for a particular position. Here is a general guide for how job negotiations might take place:

"Typically, after all the interviews are over and the company has decided who they want for the position, an HR professional will make a phone call to extend the offer. That's when the negotiation takes place. You want to be prepared for that call. You don't want that HR person to have to go back to the hiring manager with your questions, so when you're interviewing you need to have the mindset that you're going to be hired. That's when you should have asked all your questions. You want to come away from that phone call with the company's best offer. Once you feel you have that, say 'I'd like a couple of days to think about it. Can I call you on Wednesday?'"

—Cheryl Palmer, CECC, negotiation expert and president of Call to Career

NEGOTIATION PREPARATION

You can't successfully negotiate unless you know the realities of the marketplace. What is the typical salary range for the position you applied for? Does that range apply in your geographic region? And when and how do you bring this up during negotiations?

Do Your Research

Study up on salaries in your industry. You can start this research way in advance of a first interview, but by the time you've sent out your thank-yous for that interview, it's time to start getting serious about money matters. This includes:

Know what you need. How much do you pay in total monthly bills, including housing, various insurance, utilities, and groceries? What benefits do you absolutely need—such as health insurance?

Know what you can command. Your own experience, education, and other qualifications will dictate where you are on the salary scale. Be realistic in assessing what you bring to the table.

Know how your geographic area stacks up. Is the cost of living the same in your small town as it is in Manhattan? You can compare cost of living in various locations with the online calculators at Move.com (www.homefair.com/real-estate/salary-calculator.asp?cc=1) and the Cost-of-Living Wizard at MySalary.com (http://swz.salary.com/costoflivingwizard/layoutscripts/coll_start.asp).

Know the salary range for the position. This is the key element to negotiating. You need to research salaries and typical benefits by industry, position, area, and for the current economic climate. Don't worry, we're about to tell you how to do this!

Use Three Salary Sources

For good general salary information, Cheryl Palmer recommends salary.com and payscale.com.

"I also tell my clients to look for salary surveys from professional associations. Just be sure to look at more than one source, because there will be slight variations in information; consider your local geographic area. If you check three sources, you'll be pretty well armed for salary negotiation."

Find good salary info online at:

✦ Salary.com: Type in the position title and city/state you're interested in and get base salary range for free. More detailed information is available for a fee.

- Payscale.com: Identify yourself as a job candidate, job-seeker, current employee, or a business to get a free salary report based on your education/experience level, etc. The report is e-mailed to you.
- The Salary Info section on www.jobsmart.org.
- SalariesReview.com (but most information will cost a fee).
- Glassdoor.com has information from real-life employees, including salaries by industry, by occupation, and by company. Even if the company you're interviewing with is not included, this gives you some valuable comparisons.

TIP: BEFORE NEGOTIATIONS START, TRY SIMPLY ASKING THE HIRING COMPANY WHAT THE SALARY RANGE IS FOR THE POSITION. YOU CAN CALL THE HUMAN RESOURCES DEPARTMENT AND EXPLAIN THAT YOU'RE INTERVIEWING FOR THE POSITION. SEE IF THEY'LL GIVE YOU THE INFORMATION.

Practice Makes Perfect

As with interviewing skills, practicing negotiation sessions can polish your skills and prepare you like nothing else.

Palmer agrees that you should "absolutely" practice negotiating. "There's a lot of stress and a lot of pressure—mainly, pressure to just cave and accept what they offer," she warns. "You play the part of the job candidate, and have a friend or family member play the employer—or better yet, a career coach. You need someone who's going to be tough on you. It's likely the person who's offering you the job is trained in negotiation."

LIBRARY RESOURCES

If you want a tough practice partner, look for a career counselor or job coach. Some public libraries have partnerships with nonprofit career services to help job-seekers in the library; perhaps a volunteer can schedule a practice negotiation session with you.

Negotiation Checklist

Your preparations will be complete when you:

1. Have salaries or salary ranges for a comparable position from three different sources, giving you a clear picture of the package you should be offered for the job.
2. Believe those salary ranges are in line with what you need or want to earn. (If they aren't, you may be applying for the wrong jobs—or you need to rethink either your career or your budget!)
3. You have statements prepared for arguing in favor of your specific qualifications—an advanced degree, a particular skill, excellent experience.
4. You've practiced different scenarios for tough negotiations and are comfortable pressing the interviewer for what you want and deserve.

READY TO NEGOTIATE!

So: you're armed with some hard figures on what the salary range should be for the position you're being offered, you know what you need and what you want, and you've practiced some negotiation scenarios. Sounds like you're ready!

Beginning Tactics

Much like when you started interviewing for the position, you want your interviewer to give you some information before you jump in.

> "The basic rule of thumb is that whoever brings up salary first loses. The company very often doesn't want to reveal what they can pay, and the job-seeker shouldn't want to reveal what she wants."
>
> **—Cheryl Palmer, CECC, negotiation expert and president of Call to Career**

Some interviewers will simply come out and say, "This position has a salary range of $34,000 to $38,000." Most companies are likely to have salary ranges set for each position; but that doesn't mean those ranges are set in stone. "Usually HR sets the parameters for [salary and benefits], but it's driven by the budget of the department or company that's hiring," says Jill Silman, SPHR, vice president at Meador Staffing Services and a spokesperson for the Society of Human Resources Management (SHRM). So if the stated salary range isn't as high as you had expected or hoped, keep up the negotiations!

Other interviewers will ask you what you'd like to earn. It's OK to dodge the question by asking if there is a set salary range. "However, you can't continue to hedge indefinitely," says Palmer. "After you go back and forth a few times, you'll have to answer the salary inquiry. At that point, give a range, based on the research you've done. This is a good time to mention your research and the sources."

IF the salary range stated is too low and does not match your research:

+ State, "I understand that your organization has a set salary range for this position, but I'd like to make a case for increasing that range in this case."
+ Point out your salary sources and the industry averages. (Don't use your own previous or current salary as an example!)
+ Remind your interviewer of several of your top selling points, illustrating why you are a valuable candidate.
+ Don't turn down the job right away, but make it clear that you are concerned about the money offered.
+ If at this point it seems the top end of the range stated is as high as the organization will go, consider whether it's worth negotiating on other points. (See below.) If you can't get a package that suits your needs or wants, end the interview politely but try to leave the door open in case the organization's decision-makers change their minds.

IF the salary range is in line with what your research reveals:

+ Negotiate for the highest end of the range. Reiterate your selling points to show your value to the company.
+ Try for a higher salary rather than a middle-range amount with the promise of a bonus or future raise; your agreed-upon

starting salary will be set in stone, unlike promises of extra cash in the future.

✦ Even if you get the salary you wanted, continue to negotiate benefits and perks.

IF the salary range is higher than you expected:

✦ Don't express excitement or delight. You still want to negotiate the best salary and benefits you can get, so push for the higher end of the range.

✦ Consider that there may be a reason the pay is higher than usual. You may be expected to work longer hours, or travel extensively—so make sure you continue negotiations!

✦ Wait to see if the benefits package is decent. Is the higher salary range compensation for lack of health insurance or a retirement plan? If so, use your "thinking time" before accepting the offer to research how much of the high salary you'll spend making up those benefits. Is it still a good salary?

Be reasonable in your requests when you make a counter offer to the initial offer or statement. Bernice Kao, job/career specialist and job service outreach librarian at Fresno County (California) Public Library, recommends, "Lay out your counter offer two steps above the original offer. Reassure [your interviewer] of the experience and benefits you will bring." Ideally, your negotiating partner will meet you in the middle, which is what you wanted in the first place. Here's an example:

HR professional: "The Sales Associate job is what we call a 'grade 2' position, and has a salary range of $28,000 to $32,000. We think that is generous for an entry-level position."

You:	"That range seems in line with my research. I know this is an entry-level job, but I worked an internship this summer at a company like yours, so I bring some recent experience as well as my Bachelor's of Marketing, so I think I would warrant $32,000 a year."
HR professional:	"That wouldn't give you any room for a raise or cost of living increase. Why don't we say $30,000 to start."
You:	"That makes sense. But I'm confident that I can prove I'm worth more. Can we agree to schedule my first performance review for six months from my start date, with a potential raise based on my performance?"

Once you agree on salary, go on to review the benefits and perks that come with employment. These, too, are negotiable—so if the final salary offered is not what you had hoped, consider ways to make up the difference in either benefits or quality of life factors. "They've already made the offer, so see what you can get," advises Kao. "You might give them five options and they'll take three. Give them a choice, but base it in reality."

What's Negotiable?

The answer, in short, is "everything." Most job candidates focus on the size of the paycheck offered—but that's not all you can (or should) negotiate.

"It's easy to be dazzled by what appears to be a higher salary—but the total compensation package includes benefits like a retirement plan and health insurance," Palmer points out. "You have to look at that whole package."

FOR INSTANCE . . .

"One of my clients left her job in IT and got an offer that she was delighted with. She was excited about the higher salary, but when I pressed her for information on her benefits, she didn't know. She hadn't asked before she accepted the job. Well, it turned out that her previous employer had 401K matching—and the new job didn't. She was actually making *less* money."

—Cheryl Palmer, CECC, negotiation expert and president of Call to Career

---

Look at the entire package. "These things will affect your pocketbook and your life," Palmer stresses. You can negotiate:

+ Flextime / telecommuting from home
+ Health insurance: If you are already covered by your spouse, or by the military, can you negotiate a higher salary instead of health coverage?
+ Vacation time
+ When you get your first salary review (Negotiate it earlier, in hopes of getting your first raise sooner)
+ Retirement plans
+ Bonus plans
+ Tuition reimbursement
+ Stock options
+ Signing bonus
+ Relocation allowance
+ Start date

These days, more people are negotiating based on time. Parents of young children and Generation X in general value time off, so workers are bargaining for flextime, shorter days, or more days off. "Time is the new currency," says Silman.

The Final Step: Ending Negotiations

Once you and the employer have reached an agreement on all the factors of your salary and benefits package, conclude with these steps. If the negotiations occurred in person, you can state them; otherwise, it's a good idea to send in an e-mail immediately to:

+ Acknowledge the offer.
+ Make sure the terms of the offer are clear. If not, ask for clarification.
+ Thank the employer for the offer.
+ Ask for time to consider. You want to think about the job, the salary, and everything that goes with it—anywhere from overnight to two days should be acceptable.
+ Find out who you should contact with your final decision. It may be the HR person or the hiring manager.

Don't Want the Job?

It's still a good idea to ask for time to consider. You want to be certain of your decision. And if you're not happy with the final package offered, there is a slight chance that the organization may reopen negotiations.

Need More Time?

If you need more than a couple of days to consider the final job offer—such as when you are juggling more than one offer (or hope to be any day now), ask for more time. Be honest and let the employer know why you're asking for extra time, because this may be an imposition for them. It's OK to explain that you're waiting to hear about another offer, or have a follow-up interview scheduled at another company. (But keep it honest; trying to use another job offer to leverage a higher salary can backfire!)

Keep in mind that if you're requesting a lot more time than the employer has planned to make a final decision, the employer may refuse. The best practice is to pick up the phone and discuss your situation. Make it clear that you're interested in the position, but you need more time. Try to be exact in how much time.

MAKING THE DECISION

No matter how perfect the job seems, or how generous the package offered, always ask for some time to consider the offer before making a decision. This is an important step that will affect your career, your life, and your bank account, so sleep on it. Use the time you've requested to review everything you learned about the position, the organization, the salary and benefits. Be honest in assessing whether the job and the employer are good fits for you. Once you've made your decision, it's time to act:

Accepting the Offer

When you accept a job offer, even verbally, it's like signing a contract. So don't say "yes" if you are not 100 percent certain you want that job and are willing and able to take it. If you accept a job in the excitement of the offer—say, you're

swayed by a sizable salary but have second thoughts later—it will be embarrassing to back out, and can damage your personal and professional reputation.

Here's how you should formally accept the job:

1. Telephone the hiring manager or HR professional to let them know the decision—before the deadline you promised. (You should have asked whom to contact at the end of your negotiation meeting.)
2. Follow up with an e-mail message stating that you've accepted the offer, and requesting a letter of agreement or contract stating the terms agreed to.
3. Play it safe—wait until you get that letter, review it, and finalize the offer before you give notice at your current job, bow out of any other positions you may be interviewing for, or move across the country to start your new position.

Most employers have a hiring process they'll follow, which includes drafting a letter of agreement for new employees. This letter—or formal contract, in some cases—should include at least the salary and benefits you agreed to in negotiations, and perhaps other details including your start date and whom you will report to.

You should carefully review the letter, compare the terms to those in your notes, and—if all details look accurate—sign it and send it back promptly. If you find a discrepancy between what you agreed to in negotiations and what the letter states, follow these steps:

1. Make a photocopy of the letter (or print out a second copy).
2. Use a pen to note the discrepancy. You can draw a single line through any text that you want deleted, and make notes in the margins for what you'd like added.
3. Don't sign the letter. In fact, you may want to write Xs or draw a line through the signature line.

4. Draft a brief cover note explaining the changes.

5. Send the marked-up copy and the cover back to the original sender, by fax or mail, and ask about next steps.

6. If the employer does not agree with you on the final terms, it's time to either reconsider the "new" offer or request another meeting for further negotiations.

If your new employer does not provide a letter of agreement—perhaps it is a very small company, or a start-up business—you should take it upon yourself to draft one and ask your new manager to review it and sign it. It's important for both parties to understand and agree to clear terms and conditions of employment up front.

Giving Notice

Once you've officially accepted the job offer and have a signed letter of agreement from your new employer, you can safely give notice at your current job. For decades, the rule of thumb is to give two weeks' notice before leaving. This is not a law; it is an ethical practice to give your employer time to cover your responsibilities.

Give your notice in person to your immediate supervisor, and let her know your last day. You don't have to go into specifics, just that you've accepted a position with another company. And DON'T accept a counteroffer from your employer if you've already accepted a new job!

TIP: BE PREPARED FOR THE POSSIBILITY THAT THE DAY YOU GIVE YOUR NOTICE MAY BE YOUR LAST DAY OF WORK THERE. SOME COMPANIES AND DEPARTMENTS ARE CONCERNED ABOUT SECURITY OR CONFIDENTIALITY, AND MAY DECIDE NOT TO LET A DEPARTING EMPLOYEE STICK AROUND. THIS IS LEGAL, BUT KNOW YOUR RIGHTS:

+ You're entitled to be paid for all the days you've worked, and, depending on your employer's policies, any vacation or personal time you've accrued.

+ You don't have to sign anything or do anything in order to collect the pay that is owed you.

Declining the Offer

If, after you take some time to consider the final offer, you opt not to take the position, do the right thing: "Call them back. Be polite and thank them for considering you," says Palmer. Let the employer know as soon as possible. After all, that organization has a position to fill, and other candidates are eager to get the call.

To decline a job offer:

1. Call the hiring manager or HR professional to let them know your decision.

2. Follow up right away with an e-mail to that person, thanking everyone involved for their time and consideration, and restating that you are declining the offer.

3. If appropriate, give your reasons for declining—you are taking another position, or you could not reach agreement on salary or benefits. Keep this message positive, and if you can't state the real reason (you hated the hiring manager), then simply state you are declining and leave it at that.

Keep your tone professional and courteous. "Even if you decide not to take the job, leave on good terms," says Palmer. "Don't burn any bridges."

THE LAST WORD

Once you've learned how to prepare and practice for negotiating, keep those skills fresh! They will come in handy throughout your career—whether you are negotiating your first raise at your new job a year after you're hired, or angling for more responsibilities. You'll find that the more you practice negotiating, and the more you actually engage in negotiations, the better you are!

Bibliography/ Webliography

GENERAL JOB-SEARCH BOOKS

Bolles, Mark Emery, and Richard N. Bolles. *Job-Hunting Online: A Guide to Job Listings, Message Boards, Research Sites, the UnderWeb, Counseling, Networking, Self-Assessment Tools, Niche Sites.* Berkeley, CA: Ten Speed Press, 2008.

Dikel, Margaret Riley, and Frances E. Roehm. *Guide to Internet Job Searching, 2008–2009 ed.* New York: McGraw-Hill, 2008.

Doyle, Alison. *Internet Your Way To a New Job: How to Really Find a Job Online.* Cupertino, CA: Happy About, 2009.

Levinson, Jay Conrad, and David E. Perry. *Guerrilla Marketing for Job Hunters 2.0: 1,001 Unconventional Tips, Tricks and Tactics for Landing Your Dream Job.* Hoboken, NJ: John Wiley and Sons, 2009.

Shapiro, Cynthia. *What Does Somebody Have to Do to Get a Job Around Here! 44 Insider Secrets and Tips that Will Get You Hired.* New York: St. Martin's Griffin, 2008.

Whitcomb, Susan Britton. *Job Search Magic: Insider Secrets from America's Career And Life Coach.* Indianapolis, IN: JIST Works, 2006.

Yate, Martin. *Knock 'em Dead 2010: The Ultimate Job Search Guide*. Avon, MA: Adams Media, 2009.

GENERAL JOB-SEARCH WEBSITES

Job-Hunt, www.job-hunt.org.

The Riley Guide, www.rileyguide.com.

Toronto Public Library, "Career and Job Search Help Blog," http://torontopubliclibrary.typepad.com/jobhelp.

Wall Street Journal, "Careers," www.careerjournal.com.

Weddle's, www.weddles.com.

WetFeet, www.wetfeet.com.

Quintessential Careers, www.quintcareers.com.

BOOKS ON JOB FAIRS

CollegeGrad.com, "Job Fair Success," www.collegegrad.com/jobsearch/Job-Fair-Success.

Quintessential Careers, "Career Fair Tutorial," www.quintcareers.com/career_fair_tutorial.

ORGANIZATIONAL TOOLS FOR JOB HUNTS

JibberJobber, http://jobhunt.jibberjobber.com/index.php.

OCCUPATION/INDUSTRY RESEARCH WEBSITES

Bureau of Labor Statistics, "Career Guide to Industries," www.bls.gov/oco/cg.

Bureau of Labor Statistics, "Occupational Outlook Handbook," www.bls.gov/oco.

Bureau of Labor Statistics, "Occupational Outlook Quarterly," www.bls.gov/opub/ooq/ooqhome.htm.

The Career Project, www.thecareerproject.org.

Fast Company, www.fastcompany.com.

Forbes, www.forbes.com.

Fortune, http://money.cnn.com/magazines/fortune/.

Indeed. www.indeed.com.

Money, "Best Jobs in America," http://money.cnn.com/magazines/moneymag/bestjobs/2009/snapshots/1.html.

O*NET OnLine, http://online.onetcenter.org.

The Riley Guide, "Career Research Center" http://rileyguide.com/careers/index.shtml.

Vocational Information Center, www.khake.com/page5.html.

Wall Street Journal, http://online.wsj.com/home-page.

WetFeet, "Industry Profiles" and "Careers," www.wetfeet.com/careers—-industries.aspx.

BOOKS ON CHANGING CAREERS

Jansen, Julie. *I Don't Know What I Want, But I Know It's Not This: A Step-by-Step Guide to Finding Gratifying Work.* New York: Penguin, 2003.

Lore, Nicholas. *The Pathfinder: How to Choose or Change Your Career for a Lifetime of Satisfaction and Success.* New York: Simon and Schuster, Fireside, 1998.

Tieger, Paul, and Barbara Barron. *Do What You Are: Discover the Perfect Career for You Through the Secrets of Personality Type.* New York: Little, Brown, 2007.

BOOKS ON RÉSUMÉS AND COVER LETTERS

Betrus, Michael. *202 Great Cover Letters.* New York: McGraw-Hill, 2008.

Enelow, Wendy, and Louise Kursmark. *Cover Letter Magic.* Indianapolis, IN: JIST Works, 2010.

Ireland, Susan. *The Complete Idiot's Guide to the Perfect Resume.* New York: Alpha Books, 2010.

McGraw-Hill's Big Red Book of Resumes. New York: McGraw-Hill, 2002.

Whitcomb, Susan Britton. *Résumé Magic.* Indianapolis, IN: JIST Works, 1999.

Whitcomb, Susan Britton, and Pat Kendall. *e-Resumes: Everything You Need to Know about Using Electronic Resumes to Tap into Today's Job Market.* New York: McGraw-Hill, 2001.

Yate, Martin. *Knock 'em Dead Cover Letters: Great Letter Techniques and Samples for Every Step of Your Search.* Avon, MA: Adams Media, 2008.

WEBSITES ON RÉSUMÉS AND COVER LETTERS

The Damn Good Resume, www.damngood.com.

Dummies.com, "Resumes," ww.dummies.com/how-to/business-careers/careers/Resumes.html.

Dummies.com, "Cover Letters," www.dummies.com/how-to/business-careers/careers/Cover-Letters.html.

Purdue Online Writing Lab, "Cover Letters," http://owl.english.purdue.edu/engagement/index.php?category_id=34&sub_category_id=42.

The Riley Guide, "Help With Your Resume and CV," http://rileyguide.com/resprep.html.

Wall Street Journal Careers, "How to Write a Cover Letter," http://guides.wsj.com/careers/how-to-start-a-job-search/how-to-write-a-cover-letter/.

BOOKS ON NETWORKING

Benjamin, Susan. *Perfect Phrases for Professional Networking: Hundreds of Ready-to-Use Phrases for Meeting and Keeping Helpful Contacts Everywhere You Go.* New York: McGraw-Hill, 2009.

Crompton, Diane, and Ellen Sautter. *Find a Job Through Social Networking: Use LinkedIn, Twitter, Facebook, Blogs and More to Advance Your Career.* Indianapolis, IN: JIST Works, 2010.

Directory of National Trade and Professional Associations. Bethesda, MD: Columbia Books, 2007.

Encyclopedia of Associations. Thomson Gale, 2005.

Hansen, Katharine. *A Foot in the Door: Networking Your Way into the Hidden Job Market.* Berkeley, CA: Ten Speed Press, 2008.

Jacoway, Kristen. *I'm in a Job Search—Now What???: Using LinkedIn, Facebook, and Twitter as Part of Your Job Search Strategy.* Cupertino, CA: Happy About, 2010.

Levinson, Jay Conrad, and Monroe Mann. *Guerrilla Networking: A Proven Battle Plan to Attract the Very People You Want to Meet.* Bloomington, IN: AuthorHouse, 2009.

McKay, Harvey. *Dig Your Well Before You're Thirsty: The Only Networking Book You'll Ever Need.* New York: Currency Books, 1999.

Pierson, Orville. *Highly Effective Networking: Meet the Right People and Get a Great Job.* Pompton Plains, NJ: Career Press, 2009.

Vermeiren, Jan. *How to Really Use LinkedIn.* Charleston, SC: BookSurge Publishing, 2009.

WEBSITES ON NETWORKING

About.com, "Top 10 Social Media Do's and Don'ts: How (and How Not) to Use Social Media to Job Search" by Alison Doyle, http://jobsearch.about.com/od/onlinecareernetworking/tp/socialmediajobsearch.htm.

IP12's Resources by Subject, "Associations," www.ipl.org/IPLBrowse/GetSubject?vid=13&cid=7.

Kawasaki, Guy, "Ten Ways to Use LinkedIn," http://blog.guykawasaki.com/2007/01/ten_ways_to_use.html#axzz0nAh7w5bx.

Weddle's Association Directory, www.weddles.com/associations/index.cfm.

Time, "LinkedIn Tricks for Networkers, Job Hunters and Hirers" by Lisa Cullen, http://workinprogress.blogs.time.com/2007/06/07/ linkedin_tricks_for_networkers/.

WetFeet, "Blog Basics: How a Blog Can Boost Your Career" by Cara Scharf, www.wetfeet.com/Experienced-Hire/Getting-hired/Articles/Blog-Basics—How-a-Blog-Can-Boost-Your-Career.aspx.

WEBSITES ON RESEARCHING COMPANIES

Fortune, "100 Best Companies to Work for," http://money.cnn.com/magazines/fortune/bestcompanies/2010.

GlassDoor, www.glassdoor.com.

GuideStar, www2.guidestar.org.

Hoover's, www.hoovers.com.

Inc., "Top 100 Inc. 5,000 Companies by Industry," www.inc.com/inc5000/2007/lists/top100-industries.html.

Jigsaw, www.jigsaw.com.

Quintessential Careers, "Guide to Researching Companies, Industries, and Countries," www.quintcareers.com/researching_companies.html.

The Riley Guide, "How to Research Employers," www.rileyguide.com/employer.html#tutor.

U.S. Securities & Exchange Commission, "Edgar Database," www.sec.gov.

Vault.com, "Employer Reviews," www.vault.com/wps/portal/usa/companies.

Yahoo! Finance, http://finance.yahoo.com.

BOOKS ON INTERVIEWING

Beshara, Tony. *Acing the Interview: How to Ask and Answer the Questions That Will Get You the Job.* New York: AMACOM, 2008.

Burns, Dan. *The First 60 Seconds: Win the Job Interview before It Begins.* Naperville, IL: Sourcebooks, 2009.

Oliver, Vicky. *301 Smart Answers to Tough Interview Questions.* Sourcebooks, 2005.

Schuman, Nancy. *The Job Interview Phrase Book: The Things to Say to Get You the Job You Want.* Avon, MA: Adams Media, 2009.

BOOKS ON NEGOTIATING

Fisher, Roger, and William L. Ury. *Getting to Yes: Negotiating Agreement Without Giving In.* New York: Penguin, 1991.

Garlieb, Stacie. *My Job Offer Negotiation Skills Are Solid (I Think) . . . So Why Didn't I Get Anything I Asked For?* Charleston, SC: CreateSpace, 2010.

Miller, Lee E. *Get More Money on Your Next Job . . . in Any Economy.* New York: McGraw-Hill, 2009.

Pinkley, Robin L., and Gregory B. Northcraft. *Get Paid What You're Worth: The Expert Negotiators' Guide to Salary and Compensation.* New York: St. Martin's Griffin, 2003.

Wegerbauer, Maryanne. *Next-Day Salary Negotiation: Prepare Tonight to Get Your Best Pay Tomorrow.* Indianapolis, IN: JIST Works, 2007.

WEBSITES ON NEGOTIATING

GlassDoor.com.

JobStar Central, "Salary Information," http://jobstar.org/tools/salary/index.php.

PayScale.com.

Quintessential Careers, "Salary Negotiation and Job Offer Tools and Resources for Job-Seekers," www.quintcareers.com/salary_negotiation.html.

Salary.com, "Negotiation Clinic," www.salary.com/Articles/ArticleDetail.asp?part=par186.

Susan Ireland's Resume Site, "Salary Negotiation Skills," http://susanireland.com/interview/salary-pay.

Index